Relate is here for people wh[...] relationships better. We help people make sense of what's happening in their relationships, decide what they want to do and make those changes.

In addition to our respected and popular range of books, we have many other ways to support people. Our counsellors are trained professionals. You can have a local appointment with a counsellor face-to-face, on the phone or consult them online through our website. We also run counselling for children in primary and secondary schools, family counselling, and education and learning courses.

We work with couples, families and individuals. Our network reaches across England, Wales and Northern Ireland, where we are the largest provider of relationship support and sex therapy.

Find more relationship advice and information about our services on our website at www.relate.org.uk or call us on 0300 100 1234.

Julia Cole is a BACP accredited counsellor, psychosexual therapist and supervisor. She worked for Relate for 12 years and has been a counsellor for 25 years. She has worked as a counsellor for the NHS, a breast cancer charity and is currently a counsellor for the armed forces. Julia has written seven books on relationships and has previously written for many national magazines and newspapers, including being an agony aunt for *The Sunday Express* and *Essentials* magazine. She has appeared widely on TV and radio, chiefly commenting on relationships and family issues. She is married with one son and one daughter.

For Eric and John

After the Affair

How to Build Trust and Love Again

Julia Cole

relate

Vermilion
LONDON

1 3 5 7 9 10 8 6 4 2

First published in 1999 by Vermilion, an imprint of Ebury Publishing
This revised edition published by Vermilion in 2010

Ebury Publishing is a Random House Group company

Copyright © Julia Cole and Relate 1999, 2010

Julia Cole has asserted her right to be identified as the author of this
work in accordance with the Copyright, Designs and Patents Act 1988.

The Random House Group Limited Reg. No. 954009

Addresses for companies within the Random House Group
can be found at: www.rbooks.co.uk

A CIP catalogue record for this book
is available from the British Library

The Random House Group Limited supports The Forest Stewardship
Council (FSC), the leading international forest certification
organisation. All our titles that are printed on Greenpeace approved
FSC certified paper carry the FSC logo. Our paper procurement policy
can be found at www.rbooks.co.uk/environment

Mixed Sources
Product group from well-managed
forests and other controlled sources
www.fsc.org Cert no. TT-COC-2139
© 1996 Forest Stewardship Council
FSC

Printed and bound in Great Britain by
CPI Mackays, Chatham, ME5 8TD

ISBN 9780091935184

Copies are available at special rates for bulk orders. Contact the sales
development team on 020 7840 8487 for more information.

To buy books by your favourite authors and register for offers,
visit www.rbooks.co.uk

This book is a work of non-fiction. The names of people in the case
studies have been changed solely to protect the privacy of others.

Contents

Acknowledgements

I wish to express my warmest thanks to everyone who made this book possible:

To Suzy Powling, formerly of Relate, who supported and encouraged me in the writing of this book as well as helping to formulate the original idea.

To Sarah Bowler, Marj Thoburn and Derek Hill, formerly of Relate, who sponsored and supported the project.

To Julia Kellaway at Vermilion for her support towards ensuring that this updated edition reached fruition.

To Jo Frank, formerly of A P Watt, and Juliet Pickering of A P Watt, for their support in the original and updated version of this book.

A thank you to all the couples I have counselled through Relate whose experiences of the effect of affairs on their relationships inspired this book.

To my children, Adam and Hannah. And very special thanks to my husband, Peter, without whose loving support nothing could be achieved.

Introduction

I have been a counsellor and therapist for 25 years. Over this time I have worked for Relate; as part of the NHS; for women dealing with life-threatening health concerns, including breast cancer; and now as a counsellor for the military and in private practice. I have seen hundreds of couples and individuals talking about affairs. For the majority of couples an affair is devastating. Most people find it a very difficult event to recover from, and many couples do not survive the impact. In my experience, around a third of couples I see are unable to rebuild the relationship once an affair has been discovered. Their sense of trust in their partner, or even friends and relations, is often crushed or smashed. Many years ago a young man told me of the affair of his wife with a friend: 'It was as if a glass jar had been dropped on the floor and I was trying to pick up all the pieces. I knew nothing would be the same again.'

I have sat in many counselling rooms watching the tears, anger and desperation of the couple before me. And yet, some couples stay together, with a good portion I help saying that the affair brought problems to the surface and helped in the long-term. They ride the rough seas of the damage to their relationship and find a new way of relating to each other. Some affairs tell a couple that they needed to pay attention to one another, stop working too hard or spending all their time with the kids instead of their partner. All affairs are symptoms, not causes, of relationship breakdown. You may not realise this, and might even deny it, but it is the case. I have yet to counsel a couple where they went from a totally happy relationship to an affair overnight. The signs were there for the couple to read. This book aims to explain why this has happened, and then what to do once the affair has come out into the open.

Over the last 10 years I have realised that the way in which affairs are conducted has changed dramatically. Before the rise of the web and social networking sites, having an affair always meant meeting clandestinely in person and communicating via a landline or by letter. When I came to update this book, it became clear that nearly everything we took for granted about how relationships function has changed radically. Ten years ago email and the worldwide web were in their infancy. There was no Facebook, Twitter or YouTube. The idea that you could conduct your love life on your mobile phone or over the PC would have seemed unimaginable, but that is what has happened. For some people, their friends on the net are closer and more supportive than people they see every day in the flesh. We have become cyber literate and accept it as a crucial part of love and life. So it is obvious that people having affairs would use the new media. Interestingly, it is not just a matter of men and women meeting via the internet and going on to have affairs in person. Many people who have cyber relationships never meet the person they are emailing or texting, so it is possible to have all the emotional effects of an affair, without ever spending time in the same room with the person who they are in contact with. This is why this book contains a chapter entitled 'Is This an affair?' to help you decide what you think about this change of relationships.

I believe that although the mode of relating through modern technology is new, the emotional effects of finding out your partner has conducted secret relationships are the same as they have been for hundreds of years. This is because the way we attach to one another is as it has been for most of human history: we find someone we want to bond with and form an intimate relationship based on trust. If this trust is broken, it hurts. However, the chief change of relating to others over the internet or phone is the speed at which we can conduct a relationship. It is possible to meet someone, form an attachment and drop them as soon as we feel bored, often by cutting them out of our friend list on a social networking site or deleting them from our mobile phone. In the same way we can eat on the run, we can meet and drop a relationship. This raises new issues for people having affairs or discovering their partner is having one. If it is all over in a flash, did it really happen? And if this is in doubt, does it do the same damage as a more 'traditional' affair? Modern media can also allow an affair to be conducted in new ways. Sexting (sending pictures of yourself in sexy poses or erotic messages) is fashionable, as is using dating sites to look for potential partners whether you are single or not. Perhaps because these are a modern phenomenon, some people feel they cannot be described as an affair. But, as this book will tell you, the pain inflicted by many of these actions can be great. Couples can, and do, break up because of them. The long-term effect of having trust broken is the same, whether the relationship was over the PC or with a neighbour.

I have tried to distil my learning about affairs gleaned over the 25 years of my experience of counselling into this book. It is my hope that you will find it informative, supportive and enlightening, whether you have had an affair, discovered one, or tried to help a friend or relative survive an affair. Relate counsellors across the UK welcome all clients, whatever their sexual preferences, straight, gay or bisexual. Because this is an update of an earlier volume I tend to refer to heterosexual couples, but I hope that gay men and lesbians will find much of the advice helpful. This book is intended to help you make sense of an affair, and may be enough to support you through the experience. But if you need more help to unravel the reasons for an affair, Relate counselling can help you and your partner. You will find contact details on page 220. In a study of Relate clients, 98 per cent of respondents said they would recommend our services to friends and family, so Relate really can make a difference to troubled relationships.

PART I

WHAT IS TRUST?

CHAPTER 1

Building Trust

This book is about trust: what makes it work and what can break it. Most people, if asked, would say that trust is important in their relationships. Sometimes it is hard to put into words what trust actually is. In fact, many couples would probably say that they could not describe it, but knew what it felt like when it was gone. If you have ever encountered a partner you found you could not trust, you already know the pain, anger and sadness that a relationship without trust can cause. This chapter will help you to explore the nature of trust, how it affects individuals and relationships and how to cope when trust is broken – especially after an affair.

Trust is important in many different kinds of relationship – between family members, at work and in the community. For instance, in our families we need to believe that promises will be kept. At work, we need to know that our colleagues will support us and undertake their correct share of work. In our communities, we need to trust that our tax payments will be used properly to keep our roads in good shape and our bins emptied. If we are let down by a relative who does not keep a promise, discover that a work colleague is unsupportive, or find our rubbish on the doorstep for weeks, we are likely to respond by feeling angry and let down. The ability to trust, and to have that trust returned, is a crucial bond in any relationship – an emotional glue that helps us feel secure and safe.

Trust in couple relationships is especially important. You may have particular ways of thinking about trust, and each couple usually has a unique view of what trust means to them.

Perhaps you have friends who trust their partner in a way that you would never dream of. Your unique and personal view is precious. Your vision of trust is like a painting that you have both contributed to as the relationship has grown and developed. In some parts of the painting the picture will be clear. For instance, you trust him absolutely as a father to your children or you completely trust her to manage the family finances. Other parts of the picture may be less clear. You may wonder if your partner will always be faithful, or be able to keep a job. Sometimes a part of the picture will be blotted or stained by a breach of trust. Sometimes a special event sharpens your ability to trust a partner. Whatever happens in your relationship, this picture will hang like a backdrop to your partnership, helping to set the scene for how you relate to one another.

WHAT DO WE MEAN WHEN WE SAY WE TRUST SOMEONE?

Here are some people talking about what trust means to them.

Tania (36) *I knew I could trust him when he drove me home on our first date. He wasn't pushy and didn't try anything on, just dropped me off at the door. Next day he kept his promise to phone me.*

Mike (22) *I left university last year and my mum and dad have been really supportive. They helped me to set up in a new town and I know I can trust them to help me if I ask them.*

Susan (31) *I was in labour with our first son and I looked at Rob's face when I was feeling worn out. He just smiled at me. I knew he would be there to see me through.*

Philip (40) *I had a drink problem a few years ago. My wife helped me to stop drinking and was always ready to listen when I needed to talk. I trusted her advice and felt supported.*

Sammy (26) *I lent my sister £200. I wouldn't have done it if I hadn't trusted her. She's paying me back in instalments. We didn't even need to write anything down because she would never let me down.*

Frankie (56) *After my divorce, I thought I would never trust anyone again. But then I bought a puppy and I know I can trust him to lift my spirits when I'm feeling low.*

John (19) *I'm disabled and rely on my local disability support team to look after me. I couldn't get up, go to the bathroom or eat a meal without their assistance. I trust them with my whole life.*

Yvonne (62) *I had an operation last year on an arthritic knee. I was very nervous about the anaesthetic, but in the end I had to trust that the anaesthetist knew his job.*

In all these examples, the speakers talk about trust in different ways. For some of them, a personal relationship allowed them to make a judgment about the other's reliability. Mike, for instance, knew his parents well enough to be sure that they would help him. For Philip, it was a belief that another person would not let him down once they had promised to do something. These people were able to decide if a person was reliable by assessing their previous behaviour. Trust can also be confirmed by the practical actions of another. When a promise to deliver an activity or service is kept, trust can grow and flourish.

Some kinds of trust are not so much in the person themselves, but in their training and abilities. For instance, Yvonne did not know her anaesthetist personally, but she trusted in his medical qualification to do his job well. John trusts that well-trained professionals will help him cope with his disability.

It is possible, like Frankie, to trust in something that cannot return an active trust. Animals are often cited as being 'faithful' or 'loyal', but cannot realistically possess these human attributes. Nevertheless, Frankie felt she could trust her puppy because she was able to give her affection to a creature that was non-judgmental and responsive in a predictable way. Some humans could benefit from sharing these attributes!

On a larger scale, we all trust in a variety of everyday institutions such as hospitals, supermarkets, governments and so on. Of course, these are all maintained by people, so it is possible to imagine our need to trust as a huge net of connections between the individuals in these institutions, with us as purchasers and stakeholders.

HOW DO WE KNOW WHEN TRUST IS PRESENT?

Here are some key indicators that most people would accept as evidence of trust.

Reliability

Promises can be formal or informal. Some of the promises made in a wedding ceremony are formal, and are supported by the law and religious tradition. Informal promises, such as a promise to mow the grass every Saturday, can easily be broken, and often are! If a promise is honoured you are likely to feel better able to trust the person again and perhaps trust them with more responsibility next time. When your local supermarket promises to sell you only fresh food, you are likely to be a frequent shopper if they keep their promise, and buy a wider range of goods once you feel confident about their promises.

Predictability

Being 'predictable' is often seen as boring and uninteresting. In fact, it is impossible to trust unless some element of predictability is present. If, for instance, you ask your partner to bath the baby every Wednesday evening because you have a late shift at work, you need to be able to predict that they will do this. If they behave in an unpredictable way, sometimes bathing the baby and other times leaving them in a soiled nappy all evening, your sense of trust will soon take a battering. In other words, if you can predict that a person will do the same thing each time you ask, you can begin to develop trust in them.

Honesty

In most relationships, truthfulness is crucial. Dishonesty and lying undermine the very essence of trust. It is not always easy to be honest, but the trusting relationship requires honesty in order to strengthen it. For instance, Meg lied to Harry about her previous boyfriend, denying that she had slept with him. Meg then discovered she had a minor sexually transmitted infection and had to alert Harry in case she had passed it on to him. Harry took a long time to trust Meg again, reasoning that if she could lie about one issue, what else could she lie about? You may also feel that you can better trust someone who is willing to give you an honest answer to a difficult question. The person who avoids answering your question, or who flatters or tells you just what you want to hear, may offer a less painful response but also ultimately prove untrustworthy.

Loyalty

Being loyal to another is a key component of trust. Ross discovered this when he found out his wife had been arrested for shoplifting. She had been through a difficult time during the previous year, losing her job and suffering the deaths of both her mother and a close friend. Ross's wife could not explain why she had stolen the cans of food from the supermarket, but

Ross stuck by her because he felt sure her behaviour was connected to the unhappy year she had recently dealt with. He advised her to get professional help, and together they slowly recovered from a miserable time. Ross was loyal to his wife, and, as she came through her mental health problems, she realised how much she trusted Ross – and just how much trust Ross had placed in her.

Commitment

In any relationship it is important that there is a shared sense of commitment. It is especially true if trust is to grow. It is very hard to trust someone who is vague about what they expect from the future of the relationship. Lots of love songs have lyrics about loving someone until the mountains crumble or the stars leave the sky. These are fine sentiments, but real commitment is more about loving someone when they arrive at the breakfast table looking terrible or just after they tell you they have spent £300 on a new pair of trainers! In other words, commitment is about caring for someone through thick or thin, and looking beyond the mundane and ordinary ups and downs of everyday life.

Shared Boundaries

Imagine your relationship as a garden. Around your relationship garden is a fence. This fence is constructed of the things that you agree are important in order for you to maintain the relationship. Some people have very high fences. For example, Marion is very unhappy about her husband looking at other women when they are out together. Marion's idea of trust in the relationship means that her husband should not look at other women. Others have low fences. For instance, Pauline accepts that her husband has affairs, but sees this as okay as long as he comes home to her. In both cases, the boundaries of the relationship have been agreed and drawn by the partners in the relationship.

Every relationship has these boundaries. Sometimes they are clear to both partners. Often they are never openly discussed, but can become clear when one partner steps over the fence. For example, Olive always assumed that her boyfriend would give up football when he became a father. When he did not, Olive found herself questioning the basis of their whole relationship. Boundaries are also composed of shared attitudes to money, childcare, sex, work and home life and a host of personal and unique beliefs about the relationship.

Complete the following questionnaire to help you understand the way you approach trust and where you draw your personal boundaries. Make a record of each of the answers you have chosen, and then read the section that relates most to you.

1. I believe that couples should:
(a) Tell each other everything about themselves early in the relationship.
(b) Talk openly to each other, although it is okay to keep some secrets about the past.
(c) Avoid discussing the past as it can cause problems.

2. Developing a trusting partnership is:
(a) Very important. All relationships depend on shared trust.
(b) Important, but it can depend on the type of relationship.
(c) Not important. No relationship can be completely safe.

3. The way I decide to trust others is usually:
(a) By getting to know them personally very well.
(b) By learning about them from other people.
(c) By taking them at face value.

4. I know I can trust someone when:
(a) They treat me with consideration and do as I ask them.
(b) They seem to behave well with others.
(c) They seem to enjoy the same things that I do.

5. Someone can usually trust me because:
(a) I keep my promises.
(b) I hardly ever let other people down.
(c) I say they can.

6. If my partner broke my trust I would:
(a) Want to find out why.
(b) Consider ending the relationship.
(c) Definitely end the relationship.

7. When I have been let down in the past I have felt:
(a) Surprised, because I thought I knew the person well.
(b) Anxious, because I did not know how the relationship could continue.
(c) Angry, because I was deceived.

8. In situations where I have to trust that a stranger will fulfil a promise I tend to feel:
(a) Worried that things will not be done properly.
(b) Trusting, unless something goes wrong, when I may feel annoyed.
(c) Relatively unconcerned because I could always ask someone else to finish the task.

9. If a friend lets me down I tend to feel:
(a) Unhappy, but unsure how to tackle the problem.
(b) Confrontational, and would definitely raise the issue with them.
(c) That they are not a true friend, and would probably drop them.

10. The true test of a trusting relationship is:
(a) That both partners stand up for the other, even if times are tough.
(b) That both partners are straightforward and honest.
(c) That both partners can believe the other.

Mostly As

Trust is very important to you. You have high expectations of a partner and set standards that you see as crucial to the success of a relationship. You may find it hard to develop a trusting partnership quickly, usually developing a relationship over several weeks or months. You are careful about whom you trust, and unlikely to trust someone on the basis of outward appearances alone. You may have a tendency to want to be in control, and fear situations where a partner may behave in an unexpected way. Once you have grown to trust another, though, you are loyal and caring, usually very committed to making the relationship work. You are not often blown off-course by small let-downs, but could run the risk of feeling badly hurt if you are let down. You may have a slightly 'rose-coloured' outlook about relationships, expecting them to be happy without working out how to keep them alive. This could lead to a 'blind spot' about the reality of the ups and downs of relationships, causing you to overreact if a problem develops.

Marie and Alan met at an Italian class they were both attending. Alan was instantly attracted to Marie because she seemed lively and interesting, often asking questions about the class topics. Marie noticed Alan because he reminded her of her elder brother. During a coffee break, some weeks into the class, Alan asked Marie if she would have dinner with him. Marie agreed and they enjoyed a first date together.

Marie noticed that Alan asked a lot of questions about her life and past experiences. At first this seemed flattering but, after a few dates, it began to feel slightly intrusive. Alan was also very particular about meeting on time and sticking to plans they had set. On one occasion, they had bought tickets to see a play in the local park. When it began to rain on the evening of the play, Marie suggested they abandon their plans and share a meal instead. Alan insisted they attend the play, even though they were soaked to the skin.

Alan and Marie continued to go out together for several months. Marie enjoyed his company and secretly found that Alan's attentions boosted her ego. In fact, she felt that he had put her on a pedestal, and this was very flattering. Although she occasionally found his desire to control situations difficult to handle, she also valued the way he looked after and cared for her. Their first real problem developed when Marie had to work away from home for two months. Alan reacted negatively to her going away, and questioned her closely about her work colleagues. When Marie revealed that she would be with two men, Alan became very upset. They argued so much that Marie wondered if Alan did not trust her at all. She left for her business trip uncertain about the future of the relationship.

Alan is an 'A' type. He took his time in asking Marie out and then tried to make sure she was trustworthy by asking lots of questions about her life. He seeks a great deal of control in the partnership, sometimes bulldozing Marie into doing what he asks. Marie enjoys some of this because she feels cared for and safe with Alan, but is also intuitively alert to his insecurities. Alan romanticises his relationship with Marie, placing her on a pedestal, but is also unable to completely believe she will be faithful to him. The argument over her work gives vent to Alan's anxiety about Marie wanting him above all others. Unconsciously, Alan may have a lack of self-worth, believing that he is not worth staying faithful to. This produces his emotional 'policeman' that wants to keep Marie safely 'locked up' in his care. This kind of behaviour can ultimately distance a partner, as they can feel controlled and unhappy rather than secure and trusted.

Mostly Bs

You see trust as an important component in a relationship, but are likely to regard it as one attribute among others, such as physical attraction, shared interests and so on. You are tolerant in a relationship, expecting a partner to come with a history, and not overly concerned about knowing every detail of their life. You assess others by observing their behaviour with others, as well as how they behave with you. This gives you a well-rounded picture of a potential partner, allowing you to learn about them in a variety of settings. You are a practical person who is usually willing to forgive the occasional mistake, perhaps regarding it as part of normal relationships. Honest about your own shortcomings, you do not expect perfection in others. You do not tolerate lies and deceptions, however, and expect straight talking on tricky issues. You can be roused to anger if you are badly let down, and could go on to worry about the future of the partnership. Although you are not afraid to get important issues out into the open, you may sometimes feel unsure about how to proceed once the concern has been aired.

Clare and Kevin were friends long before they became lovers. They had been students at the same university, and then coincidentally moved to the same town to start work. As they knew few other people in their area they spent many evenings together, sometimes at the local pub and sometimes in their flats. Gradually they began to realise that they were attracted to each other in a way that was more than friendship. Soon they were spending most evenings and nights in each other's homes.

Clare felt content with Kevin because she had known him a long time. In fact, he had gone out with her friend for some months when they were both at university. Clare saw this as positive as she knew he had treated her friend with respect; this helped her to make a personal assessment of his character. After some months together, Clare admitted that she had once had a brief affair with a married man, but had stopped it after a few weeks because she couldn't bear the guilt she felt about her actions. Kevin asked her why she had done this, but although they talked about it for some time it was not mentioned again.

Eight months after they started their relationship they moved in together. After discussing how they would pay the bills and sorting out various shared accounts, they settled down to enjoy their partnership. Then Clare discovered that a credit card bill had not been paid and that a great deal of interest had accumulated. She tackled Kevin as soon as he came through the door after work. Kevin explained he had some financial problems, partly connected to paying off his student loan. Clare felt miserable but did not know how to begin to talk to Kevin about the problem. They spent a lonely evening in different rooms. Both Kevin and Clare wondered if they had made a mistake in moving in together. The next day, they tried to sort out the problem. They decided to seek help from the credit card company, and talked about why they had not discussed this issue before.

Clare is a 'B' type. She knew Kevin a long time before they were lovers. This gave her the chance to make a judgment about his character by observing him with others. She is willing to share her own shortcomings and is realistic about Kevin and their relationship. Both of them can discuss their feelings and thoughts reasonably openly and are willing to tolerate the other's mistakes. Clare can also be impulsive, attacking Kevin emotionally the moment she feels her trust has been misplaced. As a 'B' type she is willing to face a problem head on, but may find it hard to develop a resolution. This may be because 'B'-type people are sometimes willing to take a calculated risk on trusting another, but then react quickly when their trust appears threatened. Clare is willing to seek a way forward, but will probably now ask Kevin for a reassurance that this will not happen again. She will use her keen judgment and assessment skills to learn from this event.

Mostly Cs

You would like to trust others but have a strong defence mechanism against allowing yourself to trust. You tend to avoid developing a committed relationship with another, and may feel that relationships are 'easy come, easy go'. Perhaps you were hurt in the past by having a personal trust broken, or brought up in a family that damaged your view of trust. You tend to be unquestioning about how people behave and accept them as they are. This may lead you from one broken partnership to another, without much analysis of what has gone wrong. Your tendency to blame others for the difficulties in your relationships could mask some guilt that you find hard to acknowledge. You may begin relationships well, but find that sustaining them is a problem because you are unsure about how to show your true feelings and thoughts. Other people may regard you as a survivor and able to take care of yourself. Because of this, you may find yourself abused by others who feel that you are likely to be unaffected by a betrayal. You have the potential to care deeply for another, but may feel scared to commit in this way.

Lee and Zoë met at a club that they both attended regularly. Zoë spotted Lee at the bar and thought he looked 'good for a laugh'. On that first meeting, Zoë flirted with Lee and they danced together most of the evening. Lee asked Zoë if he could come back to her place for the night, but Zoë told him it wasn't what she wanted. Lee told her he would look for her at the club the next night. This arrangement went on for some weeks. Zoë realised she liked Lee, although she knew little about him outside of the club life they shared.

Eventually, Zoë invited Lee to her home, where they made love. In the morning as they shared breakfast together, Zoë asked Lee about his job. Lee told her he worked in a local factory and Zoë told Lee she was an assistant at an estate agents. After their breakfast, Lee said he had to leave and went straight away. Zoë felt disappointed that they would not share more of the day, but accepted the situation. The same routine carried on for a few more weeks. Lee would spend the night after they met at the club, and then leave immediately after breakfast. Zoë made a few vague attempts to get Lee to talk about his life and interests, but he dodged answering them. Zoë felt that Lee would tell her when he was ready. She also liked the air of mystery that surrounded the relationship, finding it sexually exciting.

A few weeks later, Zoë's friend told her that she thought Lee was married and that his wife had recently had a baby son. Zoë asked Lee the next time they met. With a shrug of the shoulders, Lee admitted he did have a wife and child. Zoë told him to 'get lost' and they never spoke again. Zoë was shocked, but crushed her feelings because she didn't want to lose face in front of her mates. She also reasoned that no real harm had been done because Lee's wife had never found out about them. She resumed going to the club and soon met another man she felt attracted to.

Zoë is a 'C' type. She willingly accepts Lee at face value and does not pursue his past or details about his life outside of their meeting place. For Zoë, it is enough that he finds her attractive. Although she sleeps with him, Zoë is aware that she gives away little of her real self. She keeps a tight rein on her emotions, avoiding too much emotional involvement with Lee. Lee also keeps an emotional distance from Zoë, perhaps because he fears she will find out that he is being unfaithful to his wife. Zoë's friend thought that she would be upset by the news that Lee was married, but she shows little feeling. Instead, Zoë pushes any disappointment and sadness deep inside herself.

'C' types are commonly afraid to show their true feelings. They may even find it hard to admit that they have feelings about their relationships. This is often because they do not wish to appear vulnerable with others. They may believe that vulnerability can lead to people taking advantage of them. Zoë spends little time thinking about the problems in the relationship, moving straight on to the next person. She also takes part in a sexual relationship that lacks emotional commitment. People who lack a strong sense of self-worth often mistake sex for closeness, and can use it to prevent intimacy developing. Sex without emotional investment can often stop people from trusting the other as they may find it hard to know how to balance physical intimacy with emotional closeness.

By completing this questionnaire you may have discovered that you are a particular type. Or you may have found that you do not fit neatly into any category. Many people are a mixture of the different types described above, or may change types as they move through different life experiences and ages. For instance, you may have been close to a Type C when you first started developing relationships, moving on to a Type B as you matured. You could have been a Type A at the start of a relationship, becoming a Type B when you felt more confident with your partner. Alternatively, you could switch between the different types according to the partner you are with. However, many people experience learning about trust in the manner described in the three categories (A, B and C) above.

YOUR TRUSTING RELATIONSHIP

Now that you have read about some of the different ways we develop trust, and then experience it in a relationship, use the following exercise to help you think about your own relationship and your attitude towards it. You may wish to write the statements on a piece of paper, recording your answer alongside to help you reflect on the nature of the trust in your relationship.

1   Trust is important to me because . . .
Try to imagine what would happen to your relationship if all the trust was sucked out of it. Imagine yourself replacing it step by step. What would you need to do to build the trust again? Analysing the statement in this way can help you to decide why trust is important to you.

2   I know I can trust my partner because . . .
Think about your daily routine and the things you trust your partner to do with, and for, you. For instance, you may trust your partner to set the alarm clock to wake you up; to remind you about an appointment or to phone your mother; to put petrol in the car, and so on. None of these sound very grand or important, but put together they build up a picture of reliability in a partner. You may also find it useful to think of feelings that contribute to trusting a partner, such as 'I know he will always be there for me' or 'She's patient when I try to explain my ideas'. This mixture of actions, feelings and thoughts can often demonstrate the nature of trust in a relationship in a powerful way.

3   My partner knows he/she can trust me because . . .
Reflect on the way you demonstrate your trustworthiness to your partner. Do you keep promises? Are you usually honest about your activities? Do you offer support when your partner needs it? Avoid self-deception when answering this. You may discover that your partner could easily trust you. Alternatively, you may discover that your partner would have to use a lot of guesswork to know whether you are trustworthy!

4   In our relationship we show trust for one another by . . .
Use this statement to prompt you to think about the tangible

things you do each day that illustrate a degree of trust. Do you, for instance, let your partner drive your car or spend time alone with your best friend? Do you trust them to pay bills or arrange childcare? Each relationship has a unique way of sharing trust, and you will know what that is for you. You could also think about the day-to-day closeness that you share. How do you let your partner know you care about them? Do you tell them, hug them or expect them to know simply in the way you care for them?

Once you have filled in these statements, you may begin to see a pattern emerge. You might start to understand that you tend to show trust, or expect a trusting response, in a particular way. You may realise that you expect a lot of your partner, but are less keen to demonstrate your own trustworthiness. Alternatively, you may feel that you have a well-balanced relationship or that you put a great deal into the partnership but get little response from your partner. You could also discover that the length of your relationship has an effect on your answers. For instance, you may have been in your relationship for only a few months and therefore still be learning about each other. Or you could have been together for years and think you know everything about how the relationship functions.

Now you have answered the questions, look for surprises in your answers. You can still discover surprises in most relationships, no matter how long the partnership has lasted. Did you know, for example, that you trust your partner partly because they have parents you trust? Or have you reluctantly realised that you are not as trustworthy as you thought?

YOUR IDEAL RELATIONSHIP

Next, think about your ideal trusting relationship. Imagine a perfect situation where you can have any style of relationship you like. You may like to make some notes to help you reflect on what you decide is the perfect 'trusting relationship' for you. Here are some questions to prompt your thoughts:

➤ How much freedom would you like for yourself? And how much would you like to give?

➤ How will you show trust towards one another?

➤ Does your ideal image depend upon outward appearances, behaviour, communication, commitment or something else?

➤ Would you need certain circumstances to have the ideal trusting partnership? For example, would you need financial security, marriage (or not) or the support of friends?

➤ What actions would demonstrate trust in your partnership?

Using all the notes you have made, or answers you have formulated in your mind, you can now compare your answers from the questions about the relationship you are presently in with the ideal trusting relationship you have just pictured. You may like to think about where there are gaps, and if they can be worked on in your relationship. If your partner is willing, they may find it helpful to answer the same questions so that you can compare your replies. Each partner in a couple will look at the same situation and see different ways of under-standing it. This can be an emotional strength as you can use different approaches to tackle a problem or to understand the nature of the concern.

> When Louise filled in the questions above she found that she often told her partner, Lewis, 'white lies' about the cost of her clothes. Louise loves keeping up with fashion, and buys designer labels or the latest fashion item, which means that she often overspends. Lewis and Louise keep separate

*accounts so he does not know the details of her finances.
However, they do have an agreement to divide the payment
of bills and rent equally. They each have standing orders on
their accounts to make this simpler. Louise is frequently
skint at the end of the month and sometimes borrows
money from friends to cover up her debts.*

*Using the questions, Louise realised that she was
regularly deceiving Lewis about her finances. She also
began to understand that this was subtly changing the
nature of the relationship as she was worried that her
friends would tell Lewis about her borrowing or that Lewis
would think less of her if he discovered her lies. When Lewis
filled out the questions he found it hard to say why he
trusted Louise. This made him feel that he needed to
communicate more successfully with Louise if he was to feel
able to trust her completely.*

*Together they answered the questions about their ideal
trusting relationship. They quickly saw that they often
made assumptions about how the other person viewed the
relationship. Both felt that 'open and honest communication' would be part of an ideal partnership, agreeing that
their busy lifestyles meant they did not spend sufficient
quality time together. Both Louise and Lewis found that
their answers to the questions illuminated certain habits
and ways of dealing with each other that they had begun
to take for granted in the relationship, but which had the
potential to spoil their partnership in the future.*

HOW DO WE LEARN TO TRUST?

As adults, we may think that trust is an innate skill –
something we just have as part of being human. We look at a
rotten plank in a bridge and 'just know' it would be a bad idea
to trust it to get us across a river. Trust, however, is a mixture

of abilities. Some of these are perhaps part of our evolution as human beings, while others are learnt through interaction with other people from birth. For instance, some recent experiments with babies have shown that they will not crawl over a step that appears to be over a drop. In the experiment, the babies were placed on a step that appeared to be some metres over a sheer drop. In fact, a glass plate protected the babies from falling. The babies, however, did not crawl over the glass sheet; they stopped short of what they perceived to be a dangerous fall. They may possess an innate instinct that tells them it is dangerous to proceed, but this skill is not sophisticated in children. Young people often have trouble in judging dangerous situations. For example, they may misjudge the speed of a car, stepping out into its path. Or they may accept fantasy as truth, attempting to fly down the stairs like Superman.

As we grow up, learning to make accurate judgments and predictions about the world is a crucial skill in understanding what and who to trust. We need to learn how to read the signs and take appropriate action to maintain our physical safety and mental stability. For instance, when walking home from a night out we may avoid a dark alley for fear of assault, or we may leave a job that proves much too stressful to manage. We learn to trust ourselves to make an assessment of a situation and to trust others to help us with assessments. We may watch the weather news and decide that, because the forecast is trustworthy, we will take an umbrella to the shops. We will have learnt how trustworthy the forecasters are by using an umbrella last time they said it would rain (or how untrustworthy by wearing a thick jumper on a hot day!).

Most people can be idiosyncratic about trust. For instance, you may only ever watch the news on one particular channel, believing their reporting to be more honest than the news on another station because your teacher once told you this was so. Or you may trust the goalkeeper of your local football team because he once replied kindly to your fan letter to him. In these circumstances, personal emotions and beliefs have influenced your trust. Even if the news proves to be biased, or the goalkeeper lets in goals at every match, you may still cling to your trust because you have self-esteem invested in it. The goalie wrote to you personally and perhaps the teacher was a good teacher whose classes you enjoyed. You could even rationalise your trust by saying something like, 'The goalie is just having a bad season' or 'The news is usually impartial; it's just this one report that's biased'. Everybody likes to feel that they can trust their own judgment. If we make a mistake in judgment – perhaps buying a car that lets us down or taking out the wrong pension plan – we feel foolish and embarrassed. So we learn about trusting others and trusting ourselves as we grow up.

THE BEGINNINGS OF TRUST

The beginning of understanding trust in individuals is the story of how we begin to remember. When a baby is born, it is completely dependent upon its caregiver to look after it in every respect. Not only does the baby need warmth, nourishment and physical safety, it also needs love, affection and nurturing from its parents or carers. Most parents gradually learn that a certain type of cry means the baby is asking for food, while another kind means a nappy change is due or that the baby needs a cuddle. At first, the arrival of the parent to give any of these things seems unpredictable. The baby cries because it is 'programmed' to do this, but parents are also 'programmed' to respond to the cry of an infant. As the weeks progress, the baby learns that crying brings a parent. The baby also slowly learns that when the parent leaves the room, they will return. In other words, the baby begins to make a kind of prediction about how the parent will respond. If a baby could put its thoughts into words, they might look like this:

Stage 1: 'I am making this crying noise. I wonder why?'

Stage 2: 'When I make this crying noise, that big person I like comes through the door.'

Stage 3: 'If I cry, I can get that big person to come and see me. Sometimes they give me things I need.'

Stage 4: 'Crying is good because I can let the big person know I need something.'

Eventually, crying is superseded by language, but the basic elements of prediction, and the linking of asking for help and attention with crying or calling out, become part of the baby's understanding of the world and its place in it. It can make a reasonably accurate judgment about what will happen next. This is a crucial part of trust development. You have probably already noticed that the words used to describe the main elements of trust are present even in this most basic of relationships – predictability, judgment, need, support and care are all terms that we use as adults when we think about trusting another.

When a baby and parent relationship works well, the baby can make a prediction about how its parents will behave and be right most of the time. It learns to rely upon its parents. This is trust. If the parents behave in a predictable way 95 per cent of the time, the baby learns that it can believe in and trust its parents. Instead of thinking that its mother has gone forever when she leaves the room, the baby learns to predict that she will return. Some psychologists suggest that peek-a-boo games that most parents play with babies are about developing this sense of trust. The mother reappears from behind her hands, or the baby pulls the towel away to see its father, and learns that people still exist even if they are not seen.

The key to building a sense of trust in children is that parents must behave predictably. It is very hard to develop a sense of trust if you cannot make an accurate prediction about the world.

If babies are left to cry for a very long time, they may come to believe that the parents have ceased to exist. If the baby is comforted sometimes and left to cry at other times, it may never be able to develop the 'prediction' element of trust. Adults who find it hard to trust others may behave this way because they have never acquired the ability to believe in the predictability of others. This can stem from erratic parenting experiences in childhood that have caused a child to feel that trusting others is dangerous and bound to end in disappointment.

The following table shows trust-building and trust-wrecking behaviours in childhood experiences. What we experience in childhood and in teenage years is often the template for adult behaviour, strongly influencing our relationships and choice of partner in the future.

TRUST BUILDING	TRUST WRECKING
As a baby, we have parents who respond to our needs.	As a baby, we have parents who fail to respond to our needs.
As a baby, we have carers who try to understand the personal nature of our needs and see us as an individual who requires loving nurture.	As a baby, we have carers who fail to understand the personal nature of our needs and care for us as if we were a 'number on a list' rather than as an individual.
As a baby, our needs are met in a predictable manner. Our parents come to us when we cry and give us affection as well as physical care.	As a baby, we have parents who sometimes respond to our cries, and sometimes do not. Care may also be given without affection.

TRUST BUILDING	TRUST WRECKING
As a child, fair but firm guidance is given about behaviour. Our parents explain why something is wrong. For example, the parent takes the child away from the DVD player and says, 'Don't put your toast in the DVD player because it will break and you won't be able to watch your favourite programme.'	As a child, little guidance is given about how to behave, or given in an erratic way. For instance, a mother may shout at her toddler for pushing toast into the DVD player one day and laugh at her the next day. 'Guidance' may be accompanied by physical punishment.
As we grow up, adults keep their promises to us. We feel listened to and allowed to voice an opinion.	Adults do not keep promises or provide an environment where promises can be made. We may feel that voicing an opinion would be pointless.
As a young adult we are given appropriate rules about what is expected of us. We know about times to come home, when to do homework and complete household chores. Our parents are willing to negotiate on certain issues.	As a young adult we feel too constricted and tied down by our parents. Alternatively, we may long for a firm boundary from our parents and take part in risky behaviour, such as drug taking, in an effort to gain their interest.

As the table illustrates, there are particular issues that cause problems in learning to trust in later life. No parent is perfect. There will be times when a baby cries for longer than usual because the parents are busy, or when the parents snap at their toddler because they have had a bad day at work. These events are outweighed by a pattern of caring that allows the child to feel as if the parent–child relationship is built on rock rather than sand. When a child lives with daily uncertainty, and this outweighs any positive input from a parent, their ability to trust can be damaged. Their world will feel shaky and unsure and they are likely to feel that it is not worth even attempting to trust. Children who experience this may find the development of trust too hard a task, and spend their life avoiding relationships that look for trust.

Katie could never remember a time when she felt close to her father. As an adult, looking back on her childhood, she saw her father as a frightening presence rather than a comforting one. She described him to her friends as a bully who often resorted to a slap or to name-calling. There were times, though, often after he had been drinking, when he was funny and, surprisingly, less difficult to deal with. This was the father that Katie liked, but even when he was less aggressive she could never let herself believe he could stay that way.

When Katie met Barry she really enjoyed his company. Barry liked Katie because she could be fun, but mainly because he thought he saw a side to her that others did not often realise was there. He thought that Katie was looking for a committed relationship, although others saw her as a 'good-time girl' who did not take life seriously. Katie had had lots of boyfriends, none of whom had lasted longer than a few weeks or months. Barry took Katie out and soon realised he was falling in love with her. When Barry told her how he felt, Katie took fright. She backed off, saying she wanted a break because it was 'all too heavy for her', but Barry did not take no for an answer. After some weeks of constant phone calls, Katie agreed to meet him. Barry eventually persuaded Katie to talk to him and she admitted that she could not believe that any relationship could be permanent or truly safe. She told Barry that she had never been made a promise that had not been broken. Barry told her that he would keep his promises and prove his commitment.

Katie's experience with her father has left a legacy. The legacy is that she doubts that others, especially men, will keep promises or be concerned about her for the long term. Barry may be able to convince her that he will stay around and love her, but it is likely to take some years before Katie will really accept that she has found a man she can trust. The ability to trust, to make accurate judgments and predictions, is built in the early years of life. It can either enable people to choose partners they feel content with or cast a long shadow of uncertainty over a choice of partner.

Neville was brought up in a noisy, busy family. He had five brothers and sisters, and was never short of someone to play with or talk to. Although his parents weren't particularly well off, Neville never felt the family wanted for anything important as his parents had a great sense of humour and played games with their children that entertained them for hours. Neville knew that they would support him when he needed it. His mum was very strict about keeping her promises, and would go out of her way to honour a commitment to her children. On one occasion, when Neville was about eight, he was promised a bike for his birthday. Neville got his bike, but when he was grown up he discovered that his mother had sold a piece of her deceased mother's jewellery to buy it.

When Neville met Tanya, he was quickly attracted to her warm and fun-loving personality. She seemed to have the same sense of humour as his family and also shared his passion for old motorbikes. After knowing each other for a

*year, Neville and Tanya married and eventually had two
daughters. On their tenth wedding anniversary, a friend
asked them what they thought made a successful marriage.
Neville told his friend he felt the key was that he could trust
Tanya with anything. 'She helps me to feel secure and cared
for and we know each other really well. We've had ups and
downs and our fair share of arguments, but we always
know there is a bedrock of trust to fall back on.'*

Like Katie, Neville also had a legacy from his family of origin.
He felt able to trust and believe that another person, Tanya,
was worth investing in. Neville came from a family who gave
consistent care and kept their promises, occasionally at some
cost to themselves. Although he was from a large family,
Neville had a keen sense of his own identity and knew that he
was special to his parents. All of this helped him to make a
happy marriage when he became an adult.

LOOKING BACK

Now that you have read the case studies, and answered a
number of questions about your approach to trust, you may
find it helpful to reflect on what you learnt about the nature of
trust in your family as you grew up. This is because your
experiences in childhood will influence your ability to trust in
adult relationships.

1. Do you feel that your parents or carers gave you consistent and predictable care?

No parent can give perfect care every minute of every day. You
may be able to recall particular instances when you felt let
down, but try to look at the bigger picture and decide if the
care you received was 'good enough' most of the time.

2. If your parents, or other adults, made you promises, were they usually kept?

It may be helpful to reflect on different types of promise. For instance, your parents may have forgotten to buy your favourite breakfast cereal when they promised, but kept their promise to help you through a tough exam. Looking back, some promises probably seem unimportant, while others may feel very important.

3. Do you think your parents made an effort to understand your needs?

This question is really about whether you feel that your parents were able to see things from your perspective or mainly from their own viewpoint. Children who suffer from serious neglect often do so because their carers are unable to see things from the child's point of view. In learning to trust, we need to believe that the other has a willingness to enter our world and appreciate things in the way we see them, even if they do not agree with us. Many teenagers would say that their parents can't see things their way. To some extent, this is a natural part of growing up and a desire to be an individual. If, though, a young person constantly feels blocked by a parent, they may come to believe that no-one is really capable of understanding them.

4. Did you ever have arguments with family members about trust?

Arguments about trust often arise in a family. As people move from childhood to young adulthood, arguments about broken curfews, unfinished homework and messy bedrooms are common. You could even view them as a rite of passage as you learn about trusting yourself and others. However, you could feel differently if your family repeatedly told you that you were untrustworthy or a liar. This can lead individuals to feel that behaving in a trustworthy manner is pointless because they have no real hope of being believed.

5. Did you feel that some family members were more trustworthy than others?

As you grew up you may have discovered that one parent was better at keeping promises than another. For instance, you may feel that your view of men or women has been coloured by the way your mother or father behaved towards you. Some people experience this during parental divorce when one parent promises to keep in contact but gradually stops visiting. Or you may have had a parent who promised things like expensive holidays or Christmas presents when there were no funds to deliver them. Sometimes, lack of trust in a brother or sister can also cause problems, particularly if there was favouritism in the family. If a parent favoured a brother or sister above you, you could have had the painful experience of feeling that your siblings were trusted more than you were. Alternatively, your siblings may have shown resentment towards you because you seemed to be trusted more than they were.

6. Did you suffer a major disturbance to your ability to trust a family member?

As a child you may have suffered a trauma due to ill-treatment from someone in your family. Childhood abuse – physical, mental and sexual – can leave deep scars that can seriously impair the ability of an adult to trust or receive trust from others. When someone you depend on violates your security, you can feel that nobody is trustworthy. Some people who are abused shrink from committed relationships in case they go through the same emotional pain they experienced in a previous close relationship. They may also find it hard to receive trust because they doubt the veracity of the person placing the trust in them. You may find that your ability to trust others in later life is not disturbed by a deliberate act of abuse against you, but by another kind of traumatic event. Childhood bereavement can cause problems with trust in adulthood because the bereaved person may find it hard to be close to another, fearing that if they trust them they may relive the pain of their loss all over again. Conflict-ridden parental divorce, experienced in childhood, can have a similar effect on a person.

Now that you have worked through the questions above, you may be able to see patterns in the way you have learnt about trust. For instance, you may have realised that your parents were people you felt able to trust, and who also trusted you – but parents are rarely perfect! You may have identified particular issues that you can remember arguing or puzzling over, but basically feel they gave you an understanding about trust that has served you well over the years. On the other hand you may have identified problems with trust in the family you grew up in. You may find it helpful to reflect on the effect that these problems have had on your approach to relationships. In the next chapter we will see how your learning about, and experience of, trust can affect a relationship.

CHAPTER 2

The Trusting Relationship

In this chapter, you will be able to make links between your answers to the questions in Chapter 1 and the way in which your relationship has developed. If you are not presently in a relationship, use this chapter to think about past partnerships and what you might hope for in the future.

All relationships require a degree of trust. Casual relationships, which may last only a very short time, still require trust to help them function. In fact, it could be argued that they require *more* trust since the two people involved may not know each other very well. Long-term relationships require trust as the bedrock of the relationship. The man who minutely examines every item on the supermarket receipt after his wife has been shopping (yes, it still happens!), and the woman who follows her husband to his office in case he is having an affair, are suffering from a trust deficit. Eventually, repeated behaviour of this kind drives a wedge between the couple. They will find that ordinary conversations become stilted and difficult, or that one partner ends the relationship because they cannot stand the cage they have become shut in. Trust helps couples to live together and to live without anxiety when they are parted. Without it relationships become fraught with guilt and fear.

So how does trust develop in relationships? For most people it follows a series of stages that are fairly common to people in new relationships. The length of time each stage lasts is unique to each couple and individual. Some people may make a whistle-stop tour through the different stages, while others take years to reach the last phase. It all depends on you and your approach to relationships.

STAGE 1

In this phase, you will find yourself getting to know someone. You may not yet be at the point of going out together. It may be someone you have met at a social event or seen at the local pub.

Even before you speak to them, you will make judgments about the kind of person they are. For instance, you may feel that anyone who likes the same pub as you must be okay, or the person you have spotted across the dance floor may remind you of a previous boyfriend you liked. In other words, you will bring to any new meeting an emotional suitcase full of assumptions, hopes, dreams and expectations. This will influence the way you rate trustworthiness in each other before either of you has exchanged a word.

Sometimes this is helpful. For example, a woman you meet at a concert probably likes the same band as you, so your guess about her suitability would be reasonable. At other times, your choice of partner may be skewed because you have made a misjudgment. The same woman may not be as good a choice if she really hates the band and came along just to please her friend.

You need to check out your assumptions as you get to know someone. Once introduced, you will gradually begin to form a view of their character and personality. At this stage, you will probably find yourself asking a lot of questions and answering those posed by the new person in your life. This is all part of the checking-out process, and crucial to the future of the relationship. Not only will you be learning about the person, you will also be reading their body language and what they are *not* saying as well as what they *are* willing to say.

> Bridget met Josh at a party given by her best friend. Josh approached Bridget and began asking her questions, such as who she knew at the party, how long she had known their mutual friend and what she did for a living. Bridget answered the questions, noticing that Josh hardly left space in the

conversation for her to ask about him. At the end of the evening she agreed to give Josh her phone number and they met frequently in the following few weeks. Bridget made several attempts to get Josh to tell her about himself, but he usually turned the conversation round to another topic or asked her a question of his own. After two months, Bridget ended the relationship. She felt that Josh was unwilling or unable to give her anything of himself, and she could not see a future to the partnership. Some months later she learnt that Josh had recently lost his long-term girlfriend to cancer, and that he had found it hard to discuss this issue.

In this situation, what is not said can sometimes be an indicator of a sensitive subject. Josh was clearly not ready to talk about his bereavement. Bridget intuitively picked up the clues about his lack of readiness for a new relationship, but was unable to break through the barrier Josh had erected.

Sometimes an initial belief that another is trustworthy proves to be wrong. This can occur when you have simply made a mistake in choosing to be with that person. At other times, someone may deliberately set out to mislead you. This can be a painful experience because it can undermine your confidence and prevent you from feeling secure about making the right choice next time.

Penny went out with Charlie for five months before she realised that he had duped her. She had been attracted to Charlie because he appeared, on the surface, to be charming and caring. In the first few weeks of the relationship he wined and dined her, often driving her around in his smart BMW. After a while, Penny noticed that she had begun to pay for most of their trips, often because Charlie had 'forgotten' his wallet, and the BMW seemed to be constantly 'in the garage'. Gradually Penny accepted the painful truth that Charlie was simply using her to have a good time. She ended the relationship, but found herself out of pocket for some time afterwards. Charlie had not been what he appeared to be, and Penny felt uncertain about placing her trust in another man for months afterwards.

USEFUL SKILLS AT THIS STAGE

Checking Out

Ask your potential partner or friend about themselves. Notice if they evade certain subjects or change the conversation. Make a mental note of the kind of friends they mix with, and how they behave in a group or with just one or two people. It may even help to write some of your observations down so that you can remain objective. It is easy to be swept along by romantic feelings (or pure lust!), but it is wise to reflect on whether the relationship will be good for you in the future.

The 'Why?' Question

Ask yourself why you are attracted to this person. Is it anything to do with your current circumstances? For example, you may have just broken up with a long-term partner and are seeking to soothe your wounded feelings. Maybe other people think you would be good together, but are *you* really sure about the relationship? Are there any warning signals that the relationship could mean trouble? For instance, has this person shown signs of aggression or anger that make you uncomfortable?

Use Your Intuition

Most people have a sense of intuition about others. This can feel almost physical – a tightening of the muscles in the stomach or back; hairs rising on the back of the neck; feelings of pleasure or anxiety. This kind of intuition can also help you when getting to know someone. It's not unusual for a person to say, 'I just knew they were okay' or 'I had a really bad feeling about her'. Of course, you should check out your intuitive feelings by learning more about your new partner, but intuition can often be more accurate than people allow for. Learn to pay attention to your intuitive self rather than squashing feelings that cause you discomfort or concern. A readiness to trust another may begin once you feel comfortable about your original impression of them.

STAGE 2

This is the stage that has inspired countless romantic films and love songs. A racing heart, a churning stomach and passionate feelings of longing all characterise the phase in most partnerships when you realise that this is *the one* for you. You may feel that nobody else will ever be as special or important or simply realise that, to misquote the poet Yeats, 'this is the right human face'. You could experience all of these feelings even if the relationship does not ultimately stand the test of time, or only go through the slightest fluttering of emotion in a partnership that lasts for a lifetime.

In this phase you may test your ability to trust your new partner. Alternatively, you may avoid seeing things about them that might ring a warning bell about their trustworthiness. The desire to see only the best in a potential partner can cause lovers to put their heads firmly in the sand! To some extent, this is to be expected. Without the excitement of falling in love, meeting new partners might as well be a business arrangement. Interestingly, people who take part in arranged marriages often say that they experience this phase *after* the wedding.

Research into the neurochemistry of love shows that sexual arousal and the emotions of love create a chemical response in the brain. The brain is flooded by a chemical called phenylethylamine (PEA). This produces feelings of unsteadiness, pleasure and desire. It is likely that this chemical response – along with the release of dopamine, a neurotransmitter, and oxytocin – is part and parcel of finding another irresistible. In other words, we may recognise the passion and excitement that new relationships provoke as physiological 'prompts' to help us create a new partnership.

Gradually, you will journey through this intense phase at the start of the relationship, learning about how much you can trust a new partner. Simple things such as returning phone calls, arriving on time for dates or being polite to your friends and parents will give clues to trustworthiness. More complex concerns may also come to the surface. Do they listen to you? Do they understand the importance to you of the things you value in life? Do they respond sympathetically to your worries and problems? Are they willing to enter into and share your joys and pleasures? Another way of asking this question is to ask yourself if they seem able to put themselves in your shoes. This is an important part of building trust because if your partner can understand how much a particular behaviour could please or hurt you they will be much less likely to trample on your feelings or break your trust in them.

Una and Samuel had been seeing each other for four months when Una found herself asking whether she was in the right relationship. Both Una and Samuel had been married before. Each of them had a son, and they had made some attempts to bring their children together. Una was very interested in Samuel, and had been through a passionate phase of wanting to be with him all the time. Now she felt uncertain and found herself watching him with his son. Una felt that he was too hard on his son, often demanding good behaviour when the little boy was just playing rather than being naughty. Una wondered if he would be as strict with her son if they moved in together, and was unsure if she could trust his attitude. Although she still felt a strong desire for Samuel, she cooled the relationship. It ended some weeks later because the issue of her trust of Samuel with her son altered her feelings towards him.

If Una had filled in a table about trust, like the one below, she would probably have found that the issue about her son stood out as one that demanded attention.

USEFUL SKILLS AT THIS STAGE

Lift Your Rose-coloured Glasses Occasionally

While it is natural to see your partner as the best thing since sliced bread, do try to connect with reality occasionally! Reflect on your partner's attributes. Try to decide if they are genuinely attractive or if your view of them has been highly coloured by love. For example, can you stand his passion for motorbikes once you've got over how sexy he looks in his leathers?

Try Some Test Questions

Devise a list of questions that you could ask yourself about your new partner. These will be unique to you, but could look something like this:

Question	Definitely	Maybe/sometimes	Definitely not
Does he/she always keep promises?			
Would I lend them money?			
Would I let them read my personal text messages?			
Would I feel comfortable about asking him/her to babysit my child?			
Can I tell him/her my problems?			

Place a tick in the appropriate column as you ask yourself each question. Try to be honest. Several ticks in the 'Definitely not' column could indicate that you do not know your partner well enough or that you have serious reservations about the relationship. Ticks in the 'Maybe/sometimes' column may suggest that you are still learning about your new partner and will feel more confident later. You could also have detected some concerns that you would like to talk over with them. Several in the 'Definitely' column probably means your relationship has started well, but be wary of setting your partner on a pedestal. If you have most ticks in the 'Definitely' column, but one or two in the 'Definitely not' column, there are important issues for you to discuss.

STAGE 3

If you think of the different growth stages of the trusting relationship as being like a roller coaster, this stage is the steep slide down. Stage 2 represents the climb up to the dizzying heights of desire, longing and romance. Stage 3 is the dip down as the relationship matures. For some people the slide down is not too much of a dip: it may feel like a gentle slope rather than a terrifying fall. Others will feel as if their whole world has changed. This is because it is not possible to remain at the top of an emotional mountain for ever. Eventually, you will have to descend to the mundane level and talk about necessary, but ordinary, concerns, such as how the relationship is to proceed, financial arrangements, sexual desires and feelings, and even whether the relationship should end.

This is rather like learning a language in a foreign country. If you stay a short time you may get by on gestures and the odd mispronounced word. If you intend to stay for a lengthy period of time you will want to learn more of the language. As you learn the language you will also grow to understand more about the culture and beliefs of the country. Some of the things you thought charming when you first arrived may begin to seem less so. For instance, the peace and quiet of the rural area you are staying in may turn out to be irksome when the only bus to the nearest town runs erratically and sometimes not at all. This is what happens at Stage 3. The things you found attractive and thrilling about your partner originally might appear in a very different light once you have been with them for some time.

Megan thought that Ian's ability to talk to anyone, and appear the life and soul of a party, was evidence of his warm and outgoing character. Six months later she found his loudness and his annoying habit of talking over everyone else plain irritating. She wondered how she could have seen his behaviour as attractive.

Megan had discovered a great truth about building a trusting relationship: the things that attract you carry the seeds of the things you may not like. The strong silent man who seems completely reliable may sometimes appear boring and uncommunicative. The vibrant and bubbly woman may occasionally seem restless and unable to concentrate on serious issues that are important to you.

Don't despair. Not all partnerships are destined to succeed, and you may find it impossible to stay with a partner at this stage. If you split up, it is probably for lots of good reasons. If you think you can hold on, though, try to do so. You are both creating a key building block in your ability to trust each other. You will be learning about each other as real, whole people. Yes, you will have lost some of your fantasies but you will be developing the tolerance, understanding and strength that will sustain you in the months and years ahead. Now you know the strengths and weaknesses of your partner (and perhaps yourself, as you find out more about how you respond to your partner) you can start to work on a real partnership together.

USEFUL SKILLS AT THIS STAGE

Remember the Good Times

If your time at Stage 3 seems tough, try to remember the things you have done together that were fun. Think about what attracted you to your partner and look for those characteristics again. For instance, Ellen sometimes struggled to feel close to Tony once she perceived his shyness as a lack of sociability but then she remembered the great sex they shared. When they made love, Ellen realised that Tony might be shy with others, but with her he was sensual, open and uninhibited.

Accept What You Cannot Change and Change What You Can

Some parts of an individual's personality are probably unchangeable. Traits such as being talkative, withdrawn, perceptive, easily angered and so on may be genetic, or learnt so early in childhood that they are ingrained. These are attributes that neither you nor anyone else are likely to change. Other issues, such as untidiness, not listening to you or sexual problems, may be changeable.

If you feel that you want to carry on with a relationship at Stage 3 but cannot stand the way she leaves her shoes all over the house, you should be able to talk about your annoyance and sort out a way of dealing with the problem. On the other hand, you may not be able to change the situation if you come to realise that your partner flies off the handle at the slightest provocation, and shows no sign of controlling their temper once you are an established couple. Some people can learn to control aggression, but it is usually a warning sign that the future relationship may be characterised by outbursts of anger. You should think very carefully about making a commitment to a partner if what you originally took to be assertiveness turns into aggression and violence. Violence in relationships is a complex issue, but it is usually true that once a person becomes violent towards another they are likely to repeat the behaviour. Do not fall into the trap of believing that your love will magically change them. It won't, and you run the risk of being seriously hurt, both physically and emotionally. What is more, your ability to trust will have been destroyed in the process.

STAGE 4

At this stage you are climbing back up the roller coaster. Your relationship has gone through the greatest highs and deepest lows. Now you know each other well and have experienced the different elements of each other's character and personality. If you have stayed together you will have established a solid base of trust. Gradually, you will reach an emotional plateau that feels secure. As the relationship deepens and grows further, you may again experience the passion you felt when you first met, but this will be underpinned by the depth of commitment you now share with your partner.

This stage can feel good and is usually the time when couples think about the kind of partnership they want for the future. It is not unusual for couples to choose to move in together or decide on a more permanent relationship – perhaps getting married or buying a house together. Their ability to trust one another will be sufficiently developed to maintain the partnership. The couple slowly builds on this base as they learn to trust each other over issues such as shared money, and as they negotiate about sexual matters, discuss parenting and plan for the future.

Occasionally this stage can feel tame after the excitements of Stages 2 and 3. You may wonder where the drama has gone and crave the exhausting but thrilling emotions you have been through. Some people mistake Stage 2 for 'true love', not realising that this is just the 'froth on the coffee' rather than the satisfying union that more committed love can provide.

Unfortunately, they may find the ordinariness of Stage 4 dissatisfying and repeatedly end partnerships at this point. They may actually fear commitment and avoid engaging in the hard work of creating a long-term relationship.

> *Teresa and Sally had both had previous relationships. Initially, they had been very cautious about getting together but, as the weeks passed, they felt they had never found a relationship that was so fulfilling. After almost a year, they decided to buy a flat together but started to bicker about the sort of home they wanted. Teresa wanted a garden but Sally thought it was more important to be close to their place of work. Sally wondered if she had been mistaken in choosing to be with Teresa, but gradually they came through the stage of bickering and found a flat that met their needs. They celebrated their new home by holding a party for their friends, laughing with them about the rows over the move.*

Teresa and Sally moved through the phases of their new trusting relationship to find a partnership that tolerated difference and accepted that neither of them was perfect. It is this goal that most partnerships need to reach if they are to be sustained. If you place a partner on a pedestal, seeing them as perfect, or abdicate all personal responsibility by deciding that every bad thing about the relationship is centred on your partner, you will find yourself in a relationship that is not real. It is also very difficult to build and maintain trust if you are emotionally blind to your partner's human faults and failings, or constantly watching for them to do something wrong. Learning about your partner and coming to accept that they are just like you – a mixture of different feelings, emotions and behaviours – can enable you to forgive their mistakes and love them for themselves.

There are, however, some situations that may mean you cannot accept a person just 'for themselves'. Violence, aggression and abuse are never acceptable and may mean that you should withdraw from the relationship. This is a kind of 'tough love'. You should tell your partner that unless there is a firm commitment to stop the aggression, you are going to take positive action. Make your terms very clear. For instance, if you are the recipient of violent threats, spell out very clearly that these must cease. Explain what you will do if they continue. If the threats recur, carry out the action you have promised to take. Your partner will learn that they can trust you to do exactly what you have said. This is what you want them to understand. If you give confused messages to your partner, forgiving them one day and threatening to call the police the next, they will continue to abuse you because they will not be able to trust you or believe what you say. Behaving in the way you want *your partner* to behave is called 'modelling' and can have a powerful effect on how a couple relate to each other.

USEFUL SKILLS AT THIS STAGE

Look Back to Look Forward

Now is the time to do a little reflecting. Look back over the course of your relationship and notice the good things you have shared. They may be a mutual love of touring France, eating pizza together, supporting Manchester United or watching *Coronation Street*. Whatever your shared pleasures, these can pick you up when the relationship is under pressure. If possible, build them into your daily life. If you cannot take a holiday in France, take an evening class in the language, or if a restaurant visit is too expensive, spend a messy evening creating your favourite topping for a pizza.

Now think about the things you have argued about. It is common to many types of argument for the same topics to come round again and again. Take steps to sort out these repeating differences because they can become a thorn in the flesh of a loving partnership. If you argue about money, spend an evening sorting out your bank accounts and bill payments. Talk about how much money you should spend on particular things, such as evenings out or clothes, and keep a record of your incoming and outgoing cash. It's worth doing this kind of exercise because the downward spiral of arguments on the same issues can sap the strength even from a happy relationship.

Plan Ahead

This stage is an excellent time to decide what you want for the future. You may know you want to marry or feel that you are happy to cohabit. You may both want children, or none. You may have plans to go on a world tour or buy a cottage in the country. Whatever seems important to you, talk about it and decide how to make it happen. Some plans or hopes may prove to be just pipe dreams, but others may be more practical. For instance, you may decide you want to move from rented accommodation to a house of your own. Spend some time deciding how you can make this happen by investigating mortgages, reviewing your savings and looking at local houses for sale. It can help to write your scheme down and use this as a reference point later.

Be Honest About Your Future Expectations

You may have developed a successful relationship, but discover that you each have different expectations. For example, Mike and Ruth moved in together, but ran into problems when Mike found out that Ruth did not see their relationship as long term. Mike had assumed that Ruth's agreement to share a flat with him was her way of saying that she would stay with him for the foreseeable future. Ruth, however, had never seen her agreement to live with Mike as meaning she had made a firm commitment to him; in fact, she privately wondered if she would stay as long as six months. Mike and Ruth found it very hard to resolve the issue and broke up because Ruth could not make a promise to stay. Making a straightforward statement about your expectations of the relationship can improve trust because you both know where you stand. Be wary of assumptions about how a partner thinks or feels. You could end up feeling very let down or mistrustful because you have guessed wrongly about their intentions.

Now that you have read about the four stages of the developing trusting relationship you can use your answers to the questions in Chapter 1 to consider the relationship you are presently in. You may already have discovered that you have a particular approach to trust, or that you tend to get 'stuck' at a certain stage in new relationships. For example, some people never get beyond Stage 2 or cannot move on to enjoy their relationships because they find themselves disillusioned by the relative depression of Stage 3.

THE DIFFERENT WAYS COUPLES TRUST EACH OTHER

Every couple is unique. Each has an individual way of demonstrating trust in their relationship. Some of these differences are rooted in past experience, personality, culture and the way in which the couple met. We explored many of these earlier in this chapter. There are also some common themes to the styles of trust that couples show to one another. Relate counsellors often encounter these themes when couples talk to them about their relationship problems. Read the following descriptions and case studies to consider if any of them resemble your relationship. You could also try using the exercises and suggestions to correct any potential trust problems you encounter.

THE 'TIGHT GRIP' RELATIONSHIP

This relationship is characterised by a fear of loss and anxiety about the reliability of a partner. If one partner, or sometimes both, lacks the belief that they can trust the other, they may subconsciously decide they must keep an emotional 'tight grip' on their partner. They may insist on taking them to and collecting them from every trip outside of the home, or go to great lengths to ensure that their partner is where they say they are. They may constantly text or phone to check their partner's arrival at a friend's home. Instead of an adult-to-adult relationship, this kind of partnership can feel more like a parent with a child. For the person doing the checking it can feel desperate. They may not wish to check up on their partner but feel compelled to do so before they can get on with day-to-day activities.

It is not uncommon for people who wish to maintain a tight grip on partners to justify their activities by telling themselves that they need to do this to keep the partner in line. In extreme cases they may lock doors and windows to keep a partner in or threaten them with punishment if they do not comply. For the person who has such a partner the situation can feel intolerable. They may feel unable to live a normal life, or simply believe they are not trusted to behave with honour when away from their partner.

It can also spoil the everyday experience of the couple when together. Some women in 'tight grip' relationships will become upset when their partner looks at another woman in the street or enjoys a television programme featuring an attractive woman. It is not unusual for the person who perceives themselves as not trusted to decide that if they are to be condemned for doing nothing they may as well do something. In this way the partner who is striving to control their partner will find that they have caused the very thing they are most afraid of to happen.

Fiona and Roger have been married for five years. Roger believes that Fiona deliberately attracts attention to herself by dressing provocatively. They have had many bitter arguments about this issue. Fiona has taken steps over the years to tone down her clothing by wearing sober colours and styles that are somewhat frumpy. Roger, though, is not convinced this is enough and demands that she cut her long hair because he thinks that men are attracted to women with long hair. Fiona protests, but Roger says, 'If you really loved me you would do this to prove I am the only one in your life.' Fiona loves Roger, but does not know what to do to please him. She is sure that if she allows her hair to be cut Roger will find something else to pick on. Fiona believes that Roger's problems stem from the traumatic death of his mother when he was nine, but Roger will not discuss this with her.

Some 'tight grip' relationships are not so dramatic or clear cut. This way of relating to a partner may also emerge for a short while after a problem in a relationship. For instance, Kathy hung on to her boyfriend Freddie's arm during a party because Freddie had admitted to a drunken kiss with a girl he had met at a party they had been to a few weeks earlier. Sometimes it can be an understandable response to an unhappy situation. Some couples find they go through a phase of clinging to the other if one of them has been ill or has endured bereavement.

How to Cope with the 'Tight Grip' Relationship
There are some steps you can take to prevent a 'tight grip' from strangling your partnership. Try the following to loosen the grip:

Look to the Source
It is common for the partner who is trying to appease the other to take increasingly feverish steps to stop their partner's anxiety. This approach can lead to an escalation of anxiety and tension. It does little to prevent the problem recurring because

as soon as one issue is resolved another appears to take its place. For instance, Kevin insists that Rachel should call him twice a day to let him know what she is doing. Rachel agrees, even though it interrupts her working day. Then Kevin asks her to break off a friendship he disapproves of.

An effective way to resolve this type of difficulty is to try and understand where the anxiety stems from. When Rachel asks Kevin why he wants to keep her on a tight rein, he explains that his first wife had been unfaithful a number of times during their marriage. They soon realised that Kevin's demands were motivated by the fear that Rachel could hurt him in the same way. It was a great relief to Kevin and Rachel to discover that the problem was due to Kevin's previous unhappiness rather than a major relationship issue between them. Making this kind of link can take some of the heat out of 'tight grip' relationships, allowing both partners to find a resolution that improves the partnership.

Listen to the Music as Well as the Words

Many conversations are like a song. You hear and understand the words easily, but the emotional undercurrent of the conversation is like the accompaniment that a pianist plays for a singer. For instance, the question 'Where have you been?' can have a multitude of meanings. It may simply be a question about a friend's holiday, a puzzled enquiry to a colleague who missed a meeting or an accusation from a boyfriend to his girlfriend when she is late for a date. Couples in a 'tight grip' relationship often become tangled up in the words, rather than paying attention to the emotional tune that is playing behind the words. 'Tight grip' relationships often have conversations that sound like this:

SHE: Where have you been?

HE: There you go again. You don't trust me to step outside the house, do you?

SHE: That's not fair. Anyway, why are you so guilty? If it wasn't important you would tell me where you had been. What are you hiding?

HE: I can't believe you are doing this. You know I only went to the garden centre to get a new blade for the lawnmower. I can't do the simplest things – you've never trusted me, have you?

And so on, until a major argument is in full swing, with every other time that they have argued on the same issue dragged out and dissected again.

Instead of these painful exchanges, responses to an anxious partner can attempt to address the real reason for the question. Here's a replay of the same discussion that demonstrates how attending to the tune beneath the words can help defuse the situation:

SHE: Where have you been?

HE: It sounds as if you have been worried about me.

SHE: Yes, I have. I expected you back half an hour ago.

HE: I know you find it difficult when I am later than I expected to be. Tell me why you worry about me.

SHE: I feel afraid that you may have had an accident or been hurt.

HE: I try to return at the time you expect me, but it's not always possible. If anything happens when I go out I promise to contact you as soon as I can. But you can rely on me to do what I say I will. I promised to find the new blade for the lawnmower, and here it is!

SHE: I suppose I do make a fuss and I know you keep your promises. I do trust you, but my anxiety gradually builds until I snap at you when you come home.

Here the male partner listens to and reflects back to his partner the emotion he hears beneath the question 'Where have you been?' This allows them both to tackle the real issues rather than become drawn into an argument. You may notice that he does not promise to rush home next time he is late or tell her she is being foolish. He states the truth, but emphasises that he is reliable within the context of their relationship. Of course, one conversation in this style will not solve all the problems of a 'tight grip' relationship, but it can allow for breathing room in tense situations.

THE 'OSTRICH' RELATIONSHIP

Most people know that ostriches are supposed to push their head in the sand at the first sign of trouble. The 'ostrich' relationship resembles this behaviour. The ostrich couple commonly knows there are tricky issues about trusting each other, but they ignore them in the hope that the problems will fade away. Unfortunately, this approach often means that the difficulty simply grows until it cannot be ignored any longer and causes a great deal of damage.

It's not uncommon for this kind of behaviour to happen in relationships that other people express doubts about. For instance, teenage couples who are determined to marry, despite the resistance of parents and friends, may choose to ignore the financial and practical problems associated with marriage at a very young age. This can happen because they want to prove that they are right and everyone else is wrong. Some people notice trust problems in a potential partner but decide to turn a blind eye. This can be because they cannot bear to admit they have made a mistake, or they want the partnership to fit a private dream rather than acknowledge the reality of their choice.

Lucy went out with Terry even though she knew that he had a reputation for being aggressive. She had even heard rumours that his former girlfriend had been hospitalised after a particularly vicious argument with him. When Terry started bullying Lucy she told herself that if she loved him enough he would soon stop his behaviour. Lucy did not challenge Terry. Instead, she avoided conflict when possible and placated him if he accused her of 'stepping out of line' – his term for anything he did not want Lucy to do.

Instead of the relationship improving and Terry calming down, he became even more demanding and difficult. Lucy felt she was living like a prisoner, and worse, was afraid of Terry. Rather than tackling this, Lucy went on telling herself that things would improve but they did not. After six months of fear and anxiety, Lucy decided she could not cope with Terry's moods. She packed her bags in the middle of the night and left, going to the house of a friend whom Terry did not know.

Lucy chose to ignore what she already knew about Terry – that there were serious doubts about his ability to hold down a relationship and that he might be violent. She probably did this for a number of reasons, but chiefly because she was pursuing her own idea about how the relationship would take shape. In other words, she followed a dream rather than a reality, believing that the parts of Terry she did not like could be moulded to suit her fantasy. Terry was also pursuing this agenda, attempting to make Lucy behave in the way he wanted.

In the 'ostrich' relationship this is a common occurrence. Neither partner can admit that the relationship needs to be understood in real terms. Instead, trust is developed on an insecure basis, rather like building a house on sand instead of rock. Neither partner really knows the other, and the relationship struggles under the weight of the unspoken concerns that both partners hold.

A variation on the 'ostrich' relationship can occur when a couple pushes aside matters that do not fit with their shared vision of the relationship. Some couples want to see their partnerships as romantic idylls that should not be tainted by the mundane world. They may ignore electricity bills or break off with friends who do not fit with their particular viewpoint on life.

This kind of relationship demands a great deal of emotional input from the couple, which eventually can become exhausting. They are trying so hard to ignore the things they do not wish to see, and to fashion a relationship that does not really exist, that they become emotionally overloaded. It can also lead to some practical issues not receiving the attention they deserve. Sexual problems are often ignored, as well as parenting and work concerns, simply because they do not conform to the vision the couple have of their partnership. When the problems meet the light of day, the couple can feel as if the whole basis of trust they have developed is false.

How to Cope with the 'Ostrich' Relationship

There are some simple ways to begin to tackle the 'ostrich syndrome'.

Listen to Your Intuition

At the start of the relationship, listen to your intuition. Notice the topics that are put to one side or that you feel uncomfortable discussing. A good example might be your sexual relationship, as this is an issue that many couples have difficulty discussing in depth. In a new partnership you may expect sex to 'just happen' but eventually you will need to discuss what you enjoy, when you make love, and so on. If you find that you avoid these topics, ask yourself why you are doing this.

The Communication Lucky Dip

Another approach is to try the following exercise. Write a variety of topics and issues on pieces of paper and put them in a bowl. Take it in turns to take out a piece of paper. Agree to talk about the topic on the paper for five minutes. Stick to the time limit and do this for only about half an hour at a time, once or twice a week for a couple of months. If you are unused to talking about your relationship, this will be enough at first. Avoid debates and arguments. Talk about your feelings and hunches rather than enter into a tit-for-tat exchange. Do the exercise when you are both relaxed and unlikely to be interrupted. Make sure you are sitting down and can easily maintain eye contact. Resist walking round the room or gazing over each other's shoulders. This kind of communication exercise can feel strange, even funny, but if you persevere you will find that it gradually becomes easier to talk about subjects that have previously been hard to tackle.

Here are some topics to get you started on your communication lucky dip!

➤ We always pay our bills on time. Discuss.

➤ Do you feel that you can tell me anything?

➤ Do you feel you can trust me?

➤ What do you think are the most important things about our relationship?

➤ List three things you hope for in our life together in the next three years.

➤ Is our sex life as you would like it to be?

➤ We do/do not spend enough time together. Discuss.

➤ Do you think we have a good balance between the demands of work and home life?

➤ Suggest two positive changes we could make to our love life.

➤ Do we spend too much time on the PC/games console/mobile phone?

➤ How do you feel about being a mother/father?

➤ We always agree on parenting issues. Discuss.

The list can be endless, as you can adapt the questions and statements to suit your own partnership. Try to think of issues that you hardly ever talk about. Be wary of introducing very contentious issues straightaway. Instead, talk about topics that feel reasonably safe, working up to the more difficult ones once you have got used to the idea.

This exercise can help to lessen the 'ostrich syndrome' because you have to talk about ideas and feelings that might otherwise never be discussed. Make sure that you both contribute to the topics by agreeing that you will each put five (or as many as you decide) topics in the bowl. Change the papers regularly, or add topics that come to the surface during your daily life. For instance, you might be trying to decide whether to buy a new car or go on holiday. You could add this kind of decision to the bowl as a catalyst for your discussions. Occasionally, you may wish to talk at greater length about an issue. Tell your partner how you feel and gain their agreement to do this after the exercise. Again, if you are unused to talking in this way, just spend half an hour on the topic rather than attempting an all-night discussion that may put you off talking altogether.

The 'drip, drip' approach to talking as a couple is usually much better than intense conversations that wear you both down. It is often more beneficial to have regular five- and ten-minute conversations than hours of circling the same old issue, often resolving very little, followed by long gaps in which you hardly make contact.

THE 'SCALES OF TRUST' RELATIONSHIP

Most people vary in their ability to trust their partner during the lifetime of their relationship. For instance, you may start out trusting your partner about everything, only to discover that if you let them loose with a credit card they can empty the bank account in hours! This is a normal development in most relationships and often simply reflects the strengths and weaknesses of each partner. Many couples get together by choosing someone who has the qualities they know are not so strong in themselves. For instance, Nigella chose Felix partly because he was a confident person who had little problem in mixing with others. Nigella was shy, and although she was able to make friends once she got over the first meeting, she valued Felix's ability to break the ice and introduce her to people she might never have had the courage to talk to. Some couples, though, constantly battle over who trusts whom more, sometimes competing in the trust stakes. This is like a set of scales on which each person weighs their own, and their partner's, ability to be trusted.

> *Liam and Kate have lived together for four years. They have a two-year-old son, Ben, whom they constantly argue over. Kate feels that Liam is not a good father because she thinks he lets Ben watch too much television and feeds him junk food instead of the nutritious food she leaves for him when she goes to work. Liam feels that Kate is not relaxed enough about Ben and needs to play with him more, rather than often leaving him in his playpen while she reads papers brought home from work. In their arguments, each often accuses the other of not being trustworthy enough to care for Ben. Kate frequently tells Liam that she could easily look after Ben on her own, while Liam says he could do a better job without her. The arguments leave them both feeling miserable and worn out, and cause them to do the very thing they do not want to do – ignore Ben.*

Liam and Kate have a mental set of scales in which they weigh one another, often finding the other wanting. The problem with this kind of approach to creating a trusting relationship is that so much time is spent judging and weighing the other that they never find a way to resolve the problems they are rowing about. Liam and Kate would be better served by finding a way to compromise on their problems about raising Ben than fighting over who is the better parent.

People who carry these kind of mental scales often do so because of a low sense of self-esteem. They need to feel in the right, or more trustworthy than their partner, because if they have to give up these feelings they feel uncertain about their own abilities. The more right they feel, the more they can justify their own approach or decision, and the more they can feel good about themselves. They may also be quite driven people, always chasing the right thing to do or believe. Kate is clearly a very conscientious worker and mother, and Liam may resent this. Interestingly, relationships like this also resemble a seesaw. The more a partner pushes on their end of the seesaw, the more the other partner tries to balance the seesaw by pushing hard on their end. So the more Kate becomes vociferous in her point of view, the more Liam will seek to counteract her ideas. Eventually both partners are so far apart that they cannot communicate at all.

How to Cope with the 'Scales of Trust' Relationship

There is an important reason for trying to balance the scales of trust in a relationship. If you believe you are the only one to be trusted you will burden yourself with more and more responsibility while your partner feels increasingly alienated. You could end up more like parent and child than two adults. On the emotional seesaw the way to create a balance, and prevent either of you falling off the end, is to move towards each other along the plank at the same time. In that way you will be able to see each other and communicate successfully rather than shouting to each other across an emotional void. The following approaches can be helpful:

Balance the Scales

The way to counteract this problem is to attempt to balance the scales. This means learning to value the approach that your partner takes to problems, even if you do not agree with everything they do. For instance, you may know that if your partner cleans the bathroom they will not clean the bath in the same way that you do. You may wish they would polish the taps in the careful way that you do. However, you may ignore the fact that they de-scale the showerhead, something you neglect most times you clean. One way of looking at this is to say that *together* you can be two halves or parts of a whole that is well balanced most of the time. What you find difficult your partner can do, and vice versa. Instead of fighting your corner more and more aggressively, take a step back and look at what is actually happening. Try to assess whether a shared approach could help.

Try asking yourself the following questions next time you encounter a difficulty in making your trust scales balance:

➤ What will I gain by getting my own way?

➤ What will I lose by getting my own way? (Could the answers to these two questions cancel each other out?)

➤ What is there of benefit in my partner's approach?

➤ What is there of benefit in my approach?

➤ Do I trust my partner in other areas? If so, what works in these areas that are not working in this one?

➤ Why do I have to be right?

➤ Why do I have difficulty in valuing my partner's point of view?

Your answers to these questions could help you to understand what is really going on when you have trouble trusting and believing in your partner. Kate could have asked herself the two questions about what was of benefit in her *and* Liam's approach to Ben. She might have seen that Ben actually needed caring parenting that was both serious about his welfare and allowed him to have fun at other times, and that she and Liam had different parenting skills that together contributed to his care. She might also have realised that she was working too hard and expecting too much of her partnership.

Trust Your Partner in Less Important Areas

Another way to remedy an unbalanced relationship is to try trusting your partner in areas that are less important than the issue you disagree about. For instance, you might agree to let them cook a meal, drive the car, arrange an evening out – anything that you would normally do but could be done equally well by your partner. Once you gain confidence that they are capable of undertaking particular tasks you may feel better about trusting them on the problem you are at logger-heads over.

In this chapter you have read about the way in which trusting relationships develop, and how to tackle issues that can undermine your trusting relationship. If you have tried out any of the suggestions and tasks you may have discovered that you already have a trusting relationship, or you may have found that you need to do some work on particular elements of the relationship. Part II will concentrate on what happens when trust is broken between a couple – especially in an affair.

WHEN TRUST IS BROKEN

CHAPTER 3

Why Do Affairs Happen?

The breaking of a trust is a betrayal – a betrayal not only of an individual, but also usually of a set of hopes, dreams and expectations. If you lend money to someone who refuses to repay you, you lose your plans for the money and your relationship with the debtor. Affairs are the same. If you are the person who discovers the affair, you will probably feel anger about what has actually happened and at the loss of what could have lain ahead for the relationship. It is as if a building you have been working on has come crashing down around you.

At the time of discovery, you may feel shock and sadness, anger and confusion. Later you may experience the desire for revenge, guilt, a longing for things to be okay again and shame and embarrassment that this has happened to you. You will probably not immediately be able to understand why the affair has happened. This chapter aims to explain why affairs happen – both for the person who discovers that a partner is having or has had an affair and for the person who has been unfaithful.

WHY IS IT IMPORTANT TO BE FAITHFUL?

At this point, you might ask why we – as both individuals and groups – set such store by faithfulness. Many groups of people do not believe in absolute faithfulness to one person. For instance, some African communities believe it is right to have several wives, and Mormons in parts of North America still practise polygamy. The practice of having more than one husband is relatively uncommon. Having more than one wife may be more closely linked to producing children than to the desire to have an intimate relationship. Polygamous marriages often appear to occur because the man wishes to have many children, although the desire to have sex with a younger woman (or in some cases, a virgin) cannot be ruled out.

Most couples reading this book will probably feel that having several husbands and wives is out of the question, although it is not completely unknown for couples to take a lover into their home, creating a threesome, in order to stay together for the sake of the children of the relationship. (Whether this arrangement can benefit children is difficult to say. It is possible that it could cause as much confusion and anxiety as if the parents split up.)

The majority of couples feel that once they have made a commitment they do not want their partner to make a close relationship with someone else. Most religious marriage ceremonies include references to remaining faithful to each other, and even where the relationship is not a married one most cohabitants would feel let down by a partner who had affairs.

Relate carried out a survey about affairs, their causes and effects. A quarter of the respondents reported that they had undertaken an affair. More men than women (about 30 per cent) admitted to an affair. Married couples were less likely to have affairs than people who were in a couple relationship but not living together. Interestingly, married couples were also more likely to forgive their partner in the event of an affair. Many people added personal comments to the survey findings when they sent in their responses. Perhaps the most telling one was the following: 'To anyone about to embark on an affair I would say "think twice". It's like dropping a pebble in a pool. The ripples spread wide and touch many things.'

A survey of British people found that 83 per cent thought that 'extramarital affairs are always or almost always wrong';

86 per cent of people in the same survey felt that 'faithfulness is very important for a successful marriage'. It seems clear that most people see an affair as potentially devastating to a partnership. So, given that so many people disapprove of affairs, why do they happen in the first place?

AFFAIRS – THE REAL CAUSES

When Relate counsellors meet couples who want to talk about affairs, one of the couple often begins by saying something like, 'Everything would be okay if it wasn't for the affair that he/she has just had.' They tend to mistake the affair for the root of the problem. In fact, most affairs are symptoms rather than causes of relationship problems. They often appear after a relationship has been in trouble for some time. This may have been apparent to the couple, or so hidden from both of them that the affair seems to come out of the blue. Affairs make it very clear that there is a problem in the relationship, often in an extremely painful manner.

Although each affair is unique to a particular couple there are often themes that describe affairs. If you are reading this book in order to find out more about an affair you have experienced, try to see if it fits into any of the categories below. It is possible for any affair to take elements from all the categories, but usually one theme will predominate.

A key question to ask is 'What problem in the relationship did the affair solve?' This may seem an odd question because it is hard to imagine that an affair can solve a problem. However, in the Relate affairs survey, the most common reason for having an affair (51 per cent of respondents) was because they felt neglected or in need of more attention, with 32 per cent citing communication problems as the chief difficulty. In 20 per cent of those who responded to the survey, sexual problems were the principal reason for having an affair. So if a member of the couple felt neglected or sexually frustrated, they may have looked for a solution to their problem outside the relationship. Some people even feel that if they have an affair it will stop them worrying about the problems in the partnership. In this way, the affair can seem to solve an enduring problem in the relationship. There is more about this way of under-standing affairs later in the book.

THE 'DOOR OPENER' AFFAIR

This kind of affair usually happens when a relationship is all but over. The partner who has the affair is generally looking to end the relationship and sets up a new one because they no longer feel emotionally committed to their original partner. Sometimes the partner who finds out about the affair is relieved that the relationship is over. At other times, they may have thought that the partnership was reasonably healthy and be shocked to discover that their partner wants out.

People who undertake this kind of affair often do so because they are finding it hard to tell their partner they want to end the relationship. They use the new relationship as a way of opening the door into a new life, and may never be able to explain to their first partner why they feel things went sour. In some circumstances, it is precisely this desire to escape a partnership without facing the difficult issues in the relation-ship that prompts someone to start a 'door opener' affair.

Martha and John had been living together for four years when John discovered that Martha had been seeing someone else for several weeks. John was shocked but not surprised. He and Martha had been arguing for a year over starting a family. John wanted to have children, while Martha did not. Gradually, John had noticed that Martha was less warm towards him, and he felt that the relationship was folding up. In the end, John's friend Simon told him that he had seen Martha in a pub holding hands with a man he did not know. When John confronted Martha with this, she quickly admitted her affair and told John she was moving out.

John realised that things had been unhappy for a long time and, once over the initial sadness, felt that Martha had made the right decision. John was left puzzling over why Martha had never been able to explain to him why having children was such a big issue for her, but John eventually found a new partner and went on to have a child with her.

Not all 'door opener' affairs end in such an equitable manner. Many partners resist their partner leaving and try valiantly to shut the door, even when the person concerned is sure they want to leave.

Gita and Jonathan had been married for two years when Jonathan told Gita that their marriage was over because he loved Alice. Gita was distraught at this news. They had a new baby and Gita had had a long fight with her family over marrying a man from another culture and ethnic background.

Jonathan explained that he felt unable to stay with Gita while he loved another woman. In fact, Jonathan had been seeing Alice ever since the later stages of Gita's pregnancy. Gita and Jonathan had developed problems with their sex life at this time and Jonathan had turned to Alice because she had always flirted with him at work. Soon they were having a passionate affair and Jonathan decided he had made a mistake in marrying Gita.

During the weeks following Jonathan's announcement about leaving, Gita pleaded with him to stay. She was terrified of being alone and could not believe that Jonathan had treated her as he had. Jonathan felt less and less for Gita, though, and finally left when their son was six months old. Although he continued to visit his son, he never returned to Gita. At first, she felt that she was struggling to exist, but with the help of her two sisters she rebuilt her life over the coming years.

Gita knew that there were problems – as the difficulties over their sex life indicated – but she and Jonathan did not face these. Instead, Jonathan turned to Alice as an escape route. Gita hoped that Jonathan would return and demonstrate a willingness to repair the relationship, especially as they still needed to go on being caring parents to their little son.

Have You Encountered the 'Door Opener' Affair?

Ask yourself the following questions. If you answer 'yes' to more than six of them, you could have met the 'door opener' affair in your relationship or observed it in the relationships of your friends:

➤ Have there been problems in the relationship that are (or were) hard to discuss?

➤ Did the couple experience frequent arguments on a number of issues well *before* the affair?

➤ Has one partner tried to talk about the problems, only to encounter resistance from the other partner?

➤ Has there been a desire to escape the relationship?

➤ Once the affair started, did it seem to focus thoughts about leaving the relationship?

➤ Did the person having the affair seize the opportunity to go?

➤ Did the partner who did not have the affair experience feelings of relief?

➤ Once the partner left, did the decision to leave seem absolute? (Ambivalent feelings about leaving may indicate the affair is not a 'door opener'.)

➤ Was the decision to go a surprise to the person who did not have the affair?

➤ Did the partner who had the affair find it hard to explain why it had happened?

THE 'THREE-LEGGED STOOL' AFFAIR

This is often a long-term affair that can have an unusual effect on a relationship. Most relationships resemble a two-legged stool. They wobble about as the pressures of life affect them, with one or other person taking the weight at times or sharing the load more or less evenly at others. The 'two-legged stool' can manage as long as the strains and demands of life are not too great and neither partner feels under too much pressure. However, if the load on the couple becomes too much – perhaps because of a problem from outside the couple, such as a child who gets into trouble with the police, or from inside the couple, such as money difficulties or constant rows – one partner may seek an affair. The affair comes to act as a 'third leg' that stabilises the situation. This is because the couple can ascribe all their problems to the affair while avoiding discussing the true issue.

Couples in this situation may both know about the affair but stay together, usually wrangling about the unfaithfulness of the partner in question. As a counsellor, I have often seen this from the point of view of the lover. They are frequently given promises about their boy- or girlfriend coming to live with them, only to have these broken. In fact, the couple comes to *need* the affair. It relieves the pressure on them to address the problems that led to the affair in the first place, and continues to be an outlet that helps to give vent to their frustrated emotions.

This kind of affair can go on for years. To an outsider it may seem puzzling. The couple often does not seem very happy, but cannot seem to break out of the situation. Contrary to some other types of affair, the couple's sex life may actually improve or they may feel less tense with one another. This is usually because they are not addressing the buried emotional problems that have led to the affair and are experiencing a false feeling that the problems have gone away.

A variation on this scenario is when the affair remains a secret. Generally, the partner in the affair uses the relationship with their lover as an emotional safety valve – a way in which they can release tension and forget about the problems in their partnership. They often tell their lover that they cannot leave their original relationship because of their children or other commitments. In truth, the person having the affair may actually need the different attributes of both their partner and lover, and find it impossible to choose.

The original relationship can benefit because the partner who feels under stress can relieve this by seeing their lover and returning to their partner feeling better about things. Unfortunately, this kind of affair can only have this effect as long as the lover is willing to play the game. If they start to feel used and undervalued (as often occurs) they may decide to break the secret. If this happens, all the tension that has been diverted from the main relationship may come flooding in with a vengeance. This is because the revelation of the affair is painful in itself, and the affair ceases to be a block to the other issues that the couple needs to address. These issues then return to the situation, adding to the unhappiness.

From this it may seem logical to draw the conclusion that a secret affair can be of positive value to a relationship. Unfortunately, this is rarely the case. The very fact that an affair is going on subtly alters the way in which the couple relates, so that they end up living a lie. Their relationship is like a shadow, not really existing in the real world. This can lead to the couple feeling that their emotions and experiences together are somehow false, even when the partner who is not having the affair is still in the dark about it. As a counsellor I have often met couples who have described these feelings, but who have not understood where the feelings were coming from until the partner having an affair admitted their secret.

Dawn and Victor had been married for 14 years when Dawn began an affair with Rob, whom she had met on a girls' night out with her mates. Dawn and Victor had three daughters, aged 13, 10 and 8. At first, Dawn welcomed the attention from Rob. He was outgoing and fun to be with in a way that Victor was not. Dawn had felt bored in her marriage for a number of years, often fantasising about escaping suburbia and doing something exciting. Her attempts to get Victor to go on adventure holidays or be more spontaneous in bed had fallen on deaf ears. Added to this was her frustration with her elder daughter who, Dawn felt, went out of her way to be stroppy and difficult to talk to. Dawn and Rob went out together frequently for a number of months, under the cover of her nights out with friends. Victor did not question Dawn about her evenings out: he avoided the issue because he was rather nervous of discovering she was doing things he did not approve of.

Rob began to ask Dawn to leave Victor and live with him. Dawn prevaricated, saying she could not leave her girls and that Victor would 'collapse' without her. She told Rob to be patient and that she would consider leaving Victor when 'things were easier'. Dawn found that she felt better with Victor now that she had Rob. She stopped criticising and making demands of him. In return, Victor felt that the marriage was more stable, although he often felt emotionally cut off from Dawn and uncomfortable about their lovemaking. Privately, he thought that Dawn was just 'going through the motions' rather than entering into a full sexual experience with him.

As the months went by, Rob began to feel more and more impatient. He gave Dawn an ultimatum: she must either leave Victor or finish their relationship. Dawn was horrified. She could not imagine how she would be able to manage without Rob, but felt she could not end her marriage. Then one rainy evening, Rob came to Dawn's house. Pushing his way in, he told Victor what had been going on between Dawn and him. The whole scene was traumatic. Rob, Dawn and Victor all began shouting at each other. The three daughters came down from their bedrooms and began to cry. Eventually, Rob stormed off, leaving Dawn and Victor with the wreckage of their relationship.

The transitory stability that the affair had provided came tumbling down. Dawn's eldest daughter became more withdrawn and hard to talk to. Victor withdrew into himself, hardly communicating with Dawn. Dawn felt bereft, guilty, angry and confused all at the same time. It was at this point that they came for Relate counselling. With the counsellor they attempted to untangle the reasons for the affair. It emerged that these seemed to centre around Dawn's feeling that she had married and had children when she was too young and had no chance to 'feel free and enjoy life', as she explained during one of the sessions. They did stay together, but found the two years after the revelation of the affair extremely painful.

The 'three-legged stool' affair can appear to be an answer to some couple's problems, but usually ultimately adds to an already unhappy situation.

Have You Encountered the 'Three-legged Stool' Affair?

Ask yourself the following questions. If you answer 'yes' to more than six of them, you may have encountered the 'three-legged stool' affair in your relationship or observed it in the relationships of your friends:

➤ Has the couple recently been through a difficult time, perhaps dealing with bereavement, redundancy or parenting problems?

➤ Has the couple found these issues hard to talk about?

➤ If the affair has been revealed, has the couple blamed the affair for all their troubles?

➤ If the affair has not been revealed, or in the period before it was revealed, is, or was, there a reduction in tension?

➤ Did the couple notice an improvement in their sex life?

➤ Did the affair last more than a few weeks or months?

➤ Did the partner having the affair feel a build-up in tension that was relieved by seeing their lover?

➤ Did the partner having the affair feel as if they were in an emotional bubble when they were with their lover?

➤ Has the partner who has not had the affair found himself or herself wondering how to resolve the concerns they had previously found hard to discuss?

➤ When the affair was revealed, did it feel as if the 'weight of the world' had suddenly fallen on the couple's shoulders?

THE 'REVENGE' AFFAIR

The 'revenge' affair is often short-lived, but can be a real problem for a couple to come to terms with. Usually it occurs because one member of the partnership has been hurt. To make sense of this hurt they can unconsciously decide to wound their partner in the same way that they have been hurt. At the time that the affair takes place they may not realise that this is what they are doing, but it may become obvious after a while that they allowed a 'revenge' affair to happen.

The most obvious conditions for a 'revenge' affair are when one member of a couple has had an affair and their partner wants to get their own back. Often this type of affair occurs in relationships where the partners have not been able to express their anger towards each other about an affair or where a betrayal has been discovered years after it happened. The partner who has been betrayed may feel as if their self-esteem has been smashed, but not know how to restore a positive view of themselves. They are likely to seek a way to bolster their low self-image, and often indulge in a one-night stand or short fling. Using social networking sites to set up friendships that have an online sexual content is a good example of this sort of revenge 'attack'. This can have the psychological effect of helping the person having the 'revenge' affair to feel that they are still attractive, desired and sexy – all feelings that their partner's affair has usually squashed.

It is not unusual for the 'revenge' affair to be regretted very quickly. This is often because the person having the affair suddenly realises that they have done exactly the thing that they hated in their partner. Sometimes the person having the 'revenge' affair will make sure that their partner knows all about it. They may tell them themselves, or ensure that they tell friends who will tell their partner. Occasionally they flaunt the affair, even going so far as to make sure that they are found by their partner in bed with their lover or are seen out together. The 'revenge' affair is usually showy and designed to be an emotional missile, headed straight for the heart of the partner who has broken theirs.

Very occasionally, 'revenge' affairs are kept secret. They become a private solace for a person who puts up with repeated emotional betrayals. When a partner betrays them again and again, the memory of the 'revenge' affair can act as a private support. For example, the woman whose husband had affair after affair kept to herself her memory of the man she had met and slept with at a work conference. Each time she discovered another of her husband's infidelities she reminded herself that the man she had slept with had thought her sexy and good company. This kind of 'revenge' affair can act as a defence against the pain of facing the problems in the relationship. It is rather like wearing a thick emotional overcoat to combat the chill of an unhappy partnership.

Marion and Sollie had been married for five years. To all their friends and relatives they appeared the epitome of a happily married couple. They seemed to enjoy each other's company and had two lovely children – a boy of three and a baby girl. However, Marion hid a secret from her friends. Sollie had been having an affair since the birth of their daughter. Marion had found out almost straightaway, but never discussed the discovery with Sollie. She was afraid he would leave immediately and so decided to go on pretending that all was well. She hoped he would 'see reason' and stop the affair, but this did not happen. Instead, Sollie went on meeting the woman he was having the affair with.

After several months, Marion was at her wits' end. She felt unhappy and abandoned, even though Sollie went on appearing to be a good father and husband to the outside world. Then one day she accidentally rammed a man with her shopping trolley at the local supermarket. The man, Neil, made a joke about her 'driving', and they got chatting. Marion found herself agreeing to meet him for coffee, and then drinks, at a local bar the next day. She felt her self-esteem soar. From feeling flat and lonely, she felt attractive and interesting.

Marion and Neil began to meet regularly, and Marion found herself fantasising about how Sollie would react if he saw them together. She even wondered if she could engineer an 'accidental' meeting so she could confront Sollie with Neil. When she and Neil eventually began sleeping together, she found that she was tempted to let Sollie know how good the sex was.

After 10 months of this situation, a friend asked to talk to Marion. She told Marion in a shocked tone that she had discovered that Sollie was having an affair. Marion explained that she had known for a long time, telling her friend that she was also having an affair. With this revelation, Marion decided to confront Sollie in an unusual way. She invited her husband and lover to a meal out, not telling either what she intended. Once together, she told Sollie that she had known about his infidelities for years, and that she intended to continue seeing Neil. Neil was surprised, but Sollie was amazed. Marion felt powerful and in control of Sollie. This was exciting after years of feeling that she had been at Sollie's beck and call emotionally.

Sollie spent the next few days trying to persuade Marion to give Neil up. He promised to be faithful and to stop seeing his mistress, but Marion stuck with her decision. Months later, Neil told her he could not cope with seeing her part-time, and ended the affair. This did not worry Marion as much as she had expected. In fact, she realised that her feelings for Neil had been partly based on how much she could hurt Sollie rather than on genuine affection. Marion had hurt Sollie, and they found that the various affairs had damaged their relationship a great deal. They decided to divorce two years after Marion first met Neil.

Have You Encountered a 'Revenge' Affair?

Ask yourself the following questions. If you answer 'yes' to six or more of them you may have encountered the 'revenge' affair in your relationship or in your friends' relationships:

➤ Has a partner's unfaithfulness, or other betrayal, become increasingly hard to cope with, especially if it has lasted a long period of time?

➤ Has the subject of the first affair been hard to raise with the partner who has had the affair?

➤ Has the person who has not had the first affair fantasised about hurting their partner?

➤ Has the original affair come as a complete surprise?

➤ Did the person having the first affair reveal it in a particularly insensitive way? For example, did they introduce their lover to their partner in public, or tell everybody else first?

➤ Did the person who did not have the first affair experience a slump in self-esteem when they discovered the infidelity?

➤ Did the affair restore hurt feelings of self-worth and sexual attractiveness?

➤ Has the person having the affair experienced a desire to 'show off' their lover to their partner?

➤ Has the person having the affair left tell-tale signs about the affair for the unfaithful partner to find?

➤ If the affair has been revealed, did it create feelings of pleasure to 'get back at' the partner who had been unfaithful?

THE 'NOTICE ME' AFFAIR

This kind of affair is often a one-night stand or not even a sexual affair at all. It usually occurs in relationships where the partners are having some trouble in noticing that there are significant problems, or where the couple has tried to address concerns in the past but failed. Sometimes, one person may feel that they have consistently tried to express their feelings to their partner only to have them fall on deaf ears.

The 'notice me' affair can also happen when there are particular problems with sex. The one-night stand can say, 'I want sex to meet my needs, and I have had this affair to show you how important it is.' The person who has the affair is unlikely to be looking to leave the relationship, but wants to register real unhappiness about the partnership. It is the emotional equivalent of shouting into a megaphone after normal conversation seems to have been unheard. It can also resemble a suicide attempt, or a threat of suicide. Sometimes when a person attempts suicide they do not actually intend to kill themselves. They may be desperate to receive understanding about depression or some other concern. The 'notice me' affair can perform the same task for a long-term relationship. When all else has failed, one partner may try to use a brief affair to point out how desperate they are to sort out the issues that have beset the relationship.

In some cases, the person knows they are undertaking the affair deliberately. Others may only realise why they started the affair some way into the event. Often the partner having the affair will leave clues for the other partner to discover, such as condoms in their handbag, telephone numbers on scraps of paper in their jacket pocket or easily readable e-mails.

The 'notice me' affair can also be a sexless affair in which another person is used as an emotional threat to make the couple tackle the issues they have ignored. For instance, Mike felt that his girlfriend, Katrina, was virtually ignoring him. He started to confide in Ali, one of Katrina's best friends. Although there was no sexual relationship, Katrina began to feel uncomfortable about Mike's long phone conversations with Ali and demanded he cut contact with her. In a showdown with Katrina he told her he had been 'forced' to build a friendship with Ali because Katrina was ignoring him. Although upset and angry, Katrina realised that she *had* drifted apart from Mike and took action to resolve the problems Mike felt so strongly about.

Couples can recover from the 'notice me' affair, but only if they recognise it as a strong signal of a lack of communication. Often short-lived, it can provoke great pain and anger, but may be easier to cope with than a 'three-legged stool' affair (see page 73) where problems have become intractable or entrenched. If the warning signal of the 'notice me' affair is ignored, other types of affair may follow, causing the relationship to set sail into emotionally troubled waters.

Michelle and Andrew had been married for six years. They had not had children, although Michelle had told Andrew that she wanted a baby before she reached 35. Andrew felt they had too much at stake in their careers and was privately very uncertain about ever wanting a child. Michelle and Andrew had spent several long evenings talking about the issue, never reaching a firm conclusion.

On Michelle's 34th birthday she visited a local club with friends. Andrew was away on business, and she felt lonely. In the back of her mind she was aware of her biological clock ticking, and wondered if she could ever persuade Andrew to want to be a father. When a good-looking man approached her, she found herself flirting with him, finally agreeing to leave her group of friends to spend the evening with him. At some point during the evening Michelle realised that she was going to sleep with her admirer, called Mario, and allowed herself to be driven back to his flat, where they did indeed have sex. Michelle did not think much of the sex – it was not as good as with Andrew – and, feeling guilty and miserable, she crept out in the morning without speaking to Mario.

When Andrew returned from his business trip she blurted out her behaviour. Andrew was stunned. He had trusted Michelle absolutely, and now she had betrayed his trust. They had an extremely stormy argument, during which Michelle told Andrew that she was longing to have a child, and found his attitude completely unacceptable. Over the weeks that followed, Michelle and Andrew had some very difficult conversations. Andrew told Michelle of his doubts about being a good father, while Michelle explained her desire to be a mother. They decided to seek Relate counselling to try and unravel their feelings about the affair and the decision to become parents. In this way, the affair galvanised them into taking action on their concerns.

It may be tempting to see a 'notice me' affair as a tool with which to bring an errant partner to heel. In fact, it usually adds to the problems that a couple is already grappling with, bringing anger, guilt, anxiety and a host of other painful feelings to an already unhappy situation. The best way to deal with any relationship problem is to tackle it quickly before it spirals into an affair of any kind.

Have You Encountered a 'Notice Me' Affair?

Ask yourself the following questions. If you answer 'yes' to six or more you may have encountered the 'notice me' affair in your relationship or in your friends' relationships:

➤ Has the couple encountered a particular concern that is hard to discuss?

➤ Has the person who has had the affair tried to talk to a partner, only to feel rebuffed?

➤ Has the couple found themselves drifting apart?

➤ Was the affair short-lived?

➤ Was it a sexless affair?

➤ Did the revelation of the affair cause a particularly tricky issue to come to the surface?

➤ Has the couple tried to sort out what caused the affair?

➤ Is this the first affair the couple has had to deal with?

➤ Did the person who had the affair feel guilty and ashamed shortly afterwards?

➤ Was the affair out of character for the person involved?

THE 'AVOIDANCE' AFFAIR

Strictly speaking, the 'avoidance' affair should be called 'avoidance' *affairs,* because the couple who encounter this kind of affair are likely to find themselves caught in a situation where affairs are repeated. This is because the 'avoidance' affair is all about avoiding intimacy and commitment. The person who has this kind of affair is usually afraid of being emotionally close to, and vulnerable with, a partner. Strangely, they may want to make a commitment to someone they care about, but find themselves sabotaging the very relationship they want to feel committed to. This can result in an emotional 'dance' where they find themselves becoming close to a partner, pulling away so that they are distanced, having an affair and then trying to rebuild the relationship.

Sometimes the 'dance' starts when a particular problem emerges in the relationship – perhaps an issue that places special demands on the partner who has affairs. For instance, he or she may feel under pressure to find a better job, give more time to a new baby or support a partner through an illness. At these pressure points they may feel afraid that they cannot deliver what is being asked of them and so use an affair as a diversion. They are not likely to consciously know they are doing this, but their partner will be only too well aware of the repeating patterns.

The problem for the partner is that they will like the side of the partner who is loving and attentive, but dislike the unfaithfulness. They may feel caught in an impossible conundrum – should they stick with their partner, despite their many infidelities, because they like the person who is a good partner most of the time, or end the relationship because the affairs are intolerable? Many couples in this situation feel caught in a net of unhappiness that seems to have no way out. The real tragedy of 'avoidance' affairs is that both partners are usually struggling to have a close, meaningful relationship but feel trapped in a maze. Some people who have this kind of affair describe it as an 'addiction'. They know they should not be having affairs, but feel they cannot help themselves.

Maisie had lived with Paul for a number of years. Their relationship had always been stormy because Paul had frequent affairs. They had split up a number of times and come back together after Paul's protestations that he would never have another affair. Maisie was very confused about her feelings towards Paul. On good days, she loved him and wanted a relationship with him. On bad days, often after the discovery of yet another infidelity, she wanted to end the relationship completely.

Paul felt drawn to be with Maisie: of all the women he had known, Maisie was the person he felt able to be fairly close to. To himself, he admitted he was scared of being really close to a woman. He knew that the prospect of responsibility made him anxious, and that this was also true in his working life. He changed jobs frequently, often telling Maisie he was bored or did not like the other people in his section. He also changed jobs to escape the women he had developed affairs with. Paul restlessly cruised pubs, clubs and the Internet, meeting and sleeping with the women he contacted. At times he felt ashamed of his behaviour; at others he justified it by telling himself he was 'just highly sexed' or that he didn't need Maisie.

Paul and Maisie had spent as much time apart as together, but Maisie always took him back in the end. She hated herself for not standing up to Paul or telling him she could no longer tolerate his dalliances, but ultimately she forgave him. Maisie sometimes wondered if she was as bad as Paul, avoiding closeness by putting up with his bad behaviour and not finding a man who could be faithful.

Maisie and Paul are a good example of an 'avoidance' affair. The constant infidelities of one partner can hide a basic truth: that each partner is afraid of being really intimate with the other and so they engage in a dance of closeness and intimacy followed by withdrawal. To a degree, all relationships have some of these qualities. What appears to be an intimacy difficulty for just one person can turn out to be a psychological shield for a shared difficulty.

'Avoidance' affairs often occur as a result of an inability to trust – often learnt in early life. The person who undertakes this kind of affair probably experienced trust-wrecking behaviour from their caregivers, as described in Chapter 1. They feel uncertain about how to give trust, but also about how to be trusted. This means they are continually shifting between wanting a trusting relationship and feeling afraid of being in one. Their affairs prevent them from facing the vulnerability of closeness to another person, but also supply a pseudo-intimacy by allowing them to see the encounters as real relationships. They can be very painful experiences for both partners in the relationship, and rarely result in feelings of security or being loved. Sadly, this kind of affair may prevent a committed relationship from ever developing into a successful partnership.

Have You Encountered an 'Avoidance' Affair?

Ask yourself the following questions. If you answer 'yes' to six or more you may have encountered the 'avoidance' affair in your relationship or in those of your friends:

➤ Has the relationship had repeated ups and downs?

➤ Is there a pattern to the problems in the relationship break-ups, followed by trying again?

➤ Have there been several affairs during the course of the relationship?

➤ Has the couple considered ending the relationship on more than one occasion?

➤ Does the person having the affair often find themselves in the middle of an affair without understanding why they have started another one?

➤ Has this pattern occurred in relationships other than the one that the couple is currently in?

➤ Are there periods of time when the relationship seems very good, followed by periods when it is awful?

➤ Does the person not having the affair believe they can change the behaviour of the person who has 'avoidance' affairs?

➤ Has the person who has had the affair felt under pressure in some way in the relationship?

➤ Does the person who has repeated affairs make promises about each one being the last?

THE 'EXPERIMENTAL' AFFAIR

The 'experimental' affair is probably the affair most closely linked to sex. In the Relate survey of the causes and outcomes of affairs, about 20 per cent of respondents, both men and women, said that sexual problems in their committed relationship caused them to seek an affair. This sort of affair often takes place in couples where experience of sex has been limited. The couple may have only ever made love to each other, or found sex so difficult to talk about that their lovemaking repertoire becomes mere routine.

It is a common fallacy that all affairs are about finding sex outside of the committed couple relationship. Many affairs take place for the complex reasons described in the case studies above, but the 'experimental' affair often *is* just about sex. The partner who has the affair is usually seeking to discover what sex would be like with another person, and sets out to sleep with another person from the start. Sometimes this desire is premeditated. At other times a situation presents itself for experimentation and the man or woman seizes the opportunity to try out sex with someone else.

It is common for men and women to see this kind of affair from different viewpoints. A man may tell a woman that 'it meant nothing – it was only sex'. This can backfire because the woman may wonder if he values *their* sexual relationship in the same offhand way. A man may wonder if the woman is being honest about it being 'only sex', imagining that this is an excuse for a deeper relationship. They may both question whether their whole relationship is in trouble.

Rosie and Wesley had met at school and married when they were 20. They had only had eyes for each other from the age of 14. All their friends had seen them as the 'permanent' couple in the school and also at college. Eight years on they had a baby daughter, and felt in a relationship rut. Wesley had a secure job at a local garage, while Rosie worked part-time at a supermarket. Neither of them could quite admit to the other that they felt stuck in a 'middle-aged' marriage, although they were still only 28.

Wesley enviously watched his friends as they travelled and went clubbing at weekends. He loved Rosie, but felt he had lost some important life opportunities. He and Rosie also had sexual problems. Their sex life had started well, but had run into trouble when Rosie became pregnant. Rosie went off sex and had hardly touched Wesley since the birth of their daughter. Wesley missed their sex life, even though it had sometimes seemed a bit boring. He found himself fantasising about sex with women he passed in the street, and began to sit in the park at lunchtime to watch the women walking by.

Eventually the inevitable happened. A young woman sat next to him one day. Soon they were meeting most days, and then she invited him to her home. Wesley gave in to his feelings of arousal and they had sex together. Wesley was taken aback by her openness and willingness to do things in bed that Rosie hated – such as giving him oral sex. Wesley did not feel love or affection for his new *lover. He was clear in his own mind that Rosie was still the love of his life, but he found sex very exciting with his girlfriend.*

After some months of clandestine meetings, the relationship fizzled out. Wesley never told Rosie about his affair, but gradually their sex life became more interesting. Rosie often wondered why Wesley began trying out new things in bed, and she started to enjoy the variety of their sex life. If she had known it was partly due to Wesley's experimentation with another woman she would have been devastated. The secret stayed a secret for Rosie and Wesley, but this has the potential to lead to problems if Wesley is found out at a later date.

The 'experimental' affair is not always one where the experience turns out to be 'just sex'. In fact, the genuine 'experimental' affair is quite rare. As with all affairs, it is not wise to view this kind of affair as a remedy for an ailing relationship. Although the person who has the affair may see it as transitory, this may not be the same for their partner, who is likely to feel hurt and betrayed in the same way as if the affair had lasted years. Even if the sex life of the couple seems to improve, the improvement has not been built on an honest sharing of desires and problems, but on an avoidance of dealing with the sexual issues. This can store up trouble for the future, as can the secret affair, which can act like a time bomb, waiting to wreck a relationship months or years later.

Have You Encountered an 'Experimental' Affair?

Ask yourself the following questions. If you answer 'yes' to six or more of them you may have encountered the 'experimental' affair in your relationship or in those of your friends:

➤ Has the affair followed a problem period in the couple's sex life?

➤ Does the person who had the affair describe it as 'just sex'?

➤ Has the couple had little experience in other relationships?

➤ Did the person who had the affair feel that the person they had the affair with was not as important as the sexual experience?

➤ Was the person who had the affair attracted by the physical attributes of the person they slept with rather than their character or personality?

➤ Once the 'experimental' affair took place, did the person who had the affair feel that their desire to experiment had been satisfied?

➤ Have there been any feelings of regret that the relationship took place?

➤ Did the affair cause any particular changes in the committed relationship – different sexual behaviour, for instance?

➤ Is there little or no desire to repeat the experience?

THE 'OPPORTUNISTIC' AFFAIR

The 'opportunistic' affair is often one that is the most quickly regretted, although the emotional impact once discovered can feel as intense as for any of the affairs already described. Often it is a sexual encounter between people who have seized the chance after drinking too much, found themselves together and away from home, or simply given in to a 'full on' seduction from a friend or acquaintance.

It can also be linked to the casual surfing of dating or social networking websites. A common scenario is that a partner idly looks at a site where there is access to people who are also online or looking for a connection. This can happen because a couple has had a row, or one of them feels neglected for some reason. Once online, they may tell themselves that the link to the person they are chatting with is harmless because they are not contacting them face to face. Sometimes erotic conversation takes place or an arrangement to meet develops.

The temptation to have a fling that the other partner may never discover can feel overwhelming, and the excitement of the chase can draw people in. It often feels very heady to realise that someone else, either online or in person, wants to seize the moment and embrace a passionate but brief liaison. This type of affair can feed the ego, allowing the person having the affair to feel good about themselves and attractive and sexy, attributes they believe their committed partner has not taken much notice of lately.

Mia and Alex had been together for four years. They had bought a flat together about 18 months into the relationship after deciding they wanted to make a commitment to each other. Mia's family wanted them to get married, and often tried to influence them to do this, but Mia and Alex felt they were happy as they were.

Mia and Alex had well-paid jobs, but Mia wanted to undertake an Open University course that meant studying at home for several evenings in the week and attending some tutorials away from home. She explained to Alex that this would enable her to get a promotion and eventually more money. Alex initially agreed to Mia starting the course, but reality hit him when he realised that Mia hardly sat with him in the evenings and often came to bed late. He began to feel resentful, but guilty that he felt this way. He knew he had agreed with Mia about the study, but wanted her to pay him the same attention he had always enjoyed. Mia realised that Alex was not happy, but told herself it was only for a year and that it would be worth the annoyance that Alex seemed to be showing.

One evening, when Mia was busy completing a project in another room, Alex began looking through a social

*networking site he belonged to. He noticed a friend of his
had sent introductions to another person, Lucy, whom he
vaguely remembered meeting some months before. He
clicked on her details and realised she was online. He sent
her a message, and after half an hour they were chatting.
Alex thought she looked really attractive in her photo, and
told her. Lucy replied that she thought he looked good too.*

*Alex and Lucy began to chat regularly online, exchanging
open sex talk, culminating in no-holds-barred sexual
emails. Alex saw no harm in this, and did not regard it as
an affair because he and Lucy never met in the flesh.
However, Mia did not feel this way when she later found the
e-mails by accident. She was deeply hurt that Alex had
exchanged such frank feelings and behaviour with Lucy,
and went to stay with her mother, who lived nearby, for
some time. Eventually, Alex and Mia got back together, but
Mia found it hard to trust Alex for several months.*

The 'opportunistic' affair is one that is often hard to understand and explain. People who have had one often feel they
were in a kind of trance, following a pattern of behaviour they
find difficult to make sense of to their partner. This sense of
dislocation is enhanced if it took place following a drinking
binge or drug taking. It can sometimes follow the actions of a
crowd – the lads on a stag night who pick up girls and have sex,
or women in a group egging each other on during a night out.
As in Alex's case, it can occur when least expected and online.
It can sometimes be a way of protesting about a problem in the
relationship, but often this is not understood at a conscious
level. Instead, it can seem motiveless and follow only minor
changes in a relationship, as in Mia's decision to study with the
Open University. Unfortunately, the hurt to a partnership can
be powerful, whether the relationship is in the flesh or in
cyberspace. It can even feel more painful than an affair where
someone has thought about embarking on a relationship, or

where real affection was involved, because the hurt partner may wonder how the person they cared about could have such a casual relationship.

Have You Encountered the 'Opportunistic' Affair?

Ask yourself the following questions. If you answer 'yes' to six or more, you have probably met the 'opportunistic' affair, in either your own relationship or that of someone you know:

➤ Did the affair lack premeditation or any previous negative thoughts about the committed relationship?

➤ Was the person picked to have the affair with previously completely unknown or even, in the case of online infidelity, never met in person?

➤ Were other people in a group involved in flirting with or chatting up another group while out socialising, making the idea of involvement seem acceptable?

➤ Was the person who had the affair feeling bored or lonely?

➤ Did the person who had the affair think it would not matter, or regard it as irrelevant?

➤ Was there surprise when the affair was revealed?

➤ Was the partner who did not have the affair unsurprised it had 'happened again'?

➤ Was the affair seemingly out of character?

➤ Was it fuelled by alcohol or drugs?

➤ Was it easy to break up with the person the affair was with?

➤ Did it seem hard to explain to the committed partner why it had happened?

As you read about the different types of affair, you may well have found yourself saying, 'The affair I encountered does not fit that pattern.' Many affairs do follow a particular style, but others will take elements from the different styles. For instance, an 'experimental' affair might lead on to a 'door opener' affair if the person feels that the experiment reveals much bigger problems than they had first thought. 'Revenge' affairs can also become woven into 'avoidance' affairs because the desire for revenge can lead the person to develop a serious mistrust of their partner. They may reason that their partner deserves to be deceived because of the hurt they have caused them, but this can ultimately end the relationship. In thinking about the affair you have had experience of, use the different styles to help you understand why the affair occurred and how it developed once started. In this way you can begin to make sense of the role of the affair in your relationship or in the relationships of the people you know who embark on affairs.

CHAPTER 4

Is This an Affair?

All affairs have at their heart an essential truth: they involve deception. How this deception is perceived, though, can be very different to each member of the couple. Some people see a casual fling as virtually no deception, sometimes because there were others who were also involved in the same kind of deception. The young soldier deployed away from base who has a one-night stand, or the woman at a business conference who has an intimate night with a handsome bartender, might believe that their deception is not *really* a deception because everyone else in the group was encouraging them or doing the same thing. Many people who have had an affair will consider their behaviour to be forgivable if it was a spontaneous action undertaken in association with others.

The role of alcohol and/or recreational drugs in the 'instant affair' is also important. It's not unusual to find that the person who has had the affair cites too much drink as a reason to regard the sexual contact with another man or woman as of no account because they were 'out of it' at the time they got into bed with the new partner. This can appear to justify the behaviour, or even provoke anger when their explanation is not accepted.

> *Alys and Dave had been together for five years. Alys had been married before, but Dave had never been in a previous long-term relationship. Neither of them had any children. They had bought a flat together and felt they had a reasonable relationship, although they did argue over Dave's*

passion for golf. He spent many weekends golfing, time that Alys felt he should spend with her.

Alys often went out with her girlfriends, enjoying evenings out socialising. She liked a drink, but did not regard her drinking as a problem. She drank a lot at weekends, but less during the week. One evening, following a Saturday when she had felt particularly frustrated with Dave's lack of interest in her, she enjoyed a tipsy night out at local pubs with her friends. During the evening she met Billy, an old friend she had known at school. He offered Alys a lift home but at some point he suggested they went to his house for a nightcap. Alys agreed, texting Dave to say she was staying with a girlfriend. Once at the house, Billy kissed Alys, and soon they were in bed making love. When Alys woke up the next morning she could not believe what she had done. In fact, she was not sure what they had done because of the hangover she had. Billy seemed uninterested in her, leaving her in the house while he went out to buy milk. Alys gathered her things together and took a taxi home, where she blurted out everything to Dave. Alys told him she had not intended to hurt him, that the whole thing was spur of the moment and that they should forget all about it. Dave took a different view, feeling that Alys did not understand the hurt she had caused him, and they spent a very unhappy few weeks trying to sort out what they meant to each other following this revelation.

Have a look at the following statements to see if you agree with any of them, and if you believe any of them are genuine justifications for an affair:

➤ 'I was drunk at the time and didn't know what I was doing.'

➤ 'I thought we had an open partnership that meant we could both explore other relationships.'

➤ 'I thought we were coming to the end of our relationship.'

➤ 'I missed you so much that I sought comfort with someone who reminded me of you.'

➤ 'We only kissed a few times; that's not an affair.'

➤ 'I met him/her for coffee once a week. Nothing else happened.'

➤ 'I told her/him I would never leave you so the affair has not endangered our relationship.'

➤ 'The minute you found out I broke it off.'

➤ 'Our sex life has been so bad I thought that if I had sex with a prostitute it would relieve the pressure on you to have sex when you didn't want to.'

➤ 'My mates were all doing the same thing, so I thought it wouldn't affect us because their partners all knew they did it and seemed to accept it.'

➤ 'I was so depressed I didn't really know what I was doing.'

➤ 'You were so angry with me I thought you wouldn't care.'

➤ 'It was all over in two weeks. It meant nothing to me. It's you I love.'

➤ 'We only live together. I never thought we were forever, even if you did.'

All of these types of remark have been heard in Relate counselling rooms. They often come about because of a lack of communication between the partners, plus a desire to escape the pain of facing what has happened when the affair has come out into the open. Sometimes, the person who has had the affair is desperate for it to be dismissed, for life to get back to how it was before the whole thing exploded the relationship. Unfortunately, when you have hurt your partner in this way it can often take more than a 'sorry' and a few nights of being more attentive to each other to heal broken trust. You should also consider that deceiving a partner carries a further deception – you are likely to be deceiving yourself.

The statements above all come from this sense of trying to avoid facing the truth – you did something that was not in the relationship contract you decided upon when you got together. If you have had an affair you know this feeling, no matter how much you might protest. Although your agreement of faith-fulness might not be written in stone, or even overtly talked about every day, you will know when you have stepped over the boundary. You will be denying this to yourself because of the fear of facing the music.

In a way, this is just human nature. From childhood we want to avoid being censured or accused. It may not look like it if your child has just broken the DVD player again, but children want to please their parents. This is inherent in family relationships. Children depend on their parents to provide for them; to anger a carer is against instinct because of the fear that food, warmth and affection will be withheld or, in the worst circumstances, they might be abandoned. This is why children often go to extreme lengths to avoid their parents being angry with them. They might hide the cup they broke, or deny they were involved in yet another fight with their sister or brother. It is this instinct that is activated by an affair.

If you have had an affair, the desire to avoid trouble with a partner goes back to these primitive anxieties, even if you do not consciously realise this in your adult relationship. Your denial is the response to the fear of being found wanting, and the greater fear of the attachment to the partner being broken. Strangely, this can even be true if you are unhappy in the relationship and want to leave. This is because of the nature of adult attachments. It is not easy to end an attachment, even if it has become a relationship you no longer choose to be in. At some time in the future, you might feel relieved it is over, but at the moment when you have to admit to an affair, you are very likely to be defensive or deny the impact of the relationship.

If you are dealing with a partner who is making statements similar to those above, you may feel totally confused. They have deceived you, but it now sounds as if they did not know they were deceiving you! This is because they are trying to hold different parts of the relationship in tension – the desire to avoid your anger or sorrow, to duck the guilt that will soon hit them and also to hang on to the pleasure of the affair. This has links to the 'box effect' (see page 143) in which parts of life get 'boxed up' as if they do not exist during an affair. If you meet this experience – whether you had a relationship outside of your committed partnership or are the one discovering what has happened – you will have to ask yourself 'Was this an affair?' If it was, you will need to think about the effect it is going to have on your relationship from now on.

WHAT CONSTITUTES A DECEPTION?

In the last 10 years, a revolution has occurred. From the simple mobile phone calls of a decade ago, we can now be in almost constant contact wherever we are. Texting, picture messaging, Skype, e-mail, social networking sites and Internet forums – the list is endless. Contact with other people is streaming into our lives 24/7. This is great for most of us. We can stay in touch with family and friends in a way unthinkable to our parents and grandparents. We can arrange to meet at the drop of a hat, enjoying a spontaneity that was never possible before this new world. Via social networking websites we can even tell the world what we had for breakfast if we feel like it. So our network of possible relationships has got wider and wider, limited only by our ability to deal with and afford the technology and the time available to devote to keeping the contacts going. However, it has also caused a headache in couple relationships.

The availability of this constant contact has greatly increased the chances to have relationships outside of the committed relationship, and the range of ways to deceive a partner. Many couples are lagging behind in understanding the implications of modern technology. Individuals discovered sending texts to a girl/boyfriend (whom they may never have met in the flesh) can be genuinely surprised that their partner is upset. They may say something like, 'It's only a text – nothing for you to worry about.'

Why is phone, e-mail or text sex attractive? Men and women who do this often report excitement, arousal and a sense of guilty pleasure at using mobiles or computers to send explicit messages to people they probably should not be writing to. It also has elements of incongruity – receiving a sexed-up message on a crowded commuter train can cause the recipient to look around and tell themselves they are not as boring or unattractive as everyone else on the 8.12 from Guildford! (Of course, for all they know, everyone else in the carriage is also exchanging randy messages with a lover!) It can therefore make you feel special and sexually knowing.

In the Relate affairs survey, 51 per cent of people who'd had an affair said it was because they felt neglected or lacking in attention. This is the biggest clue to the prevalence of texting and e-mailing in affairs – they are an instant self-esteem boost and accessible anywhere. Developing this in your committed partnership could help to avoid feelings of neglect.

In previous generations, if you wanted an affair you had to physically leave your home and go somewhere to meet others. It probably took planning, and time, to accomplish. Now you can unlock the laptop and exchange sexual e-mails with someone you fancy on a dating website in just a few minutes. So how do you decide what constitutes an affair or betrayal?

This questionnaire will help you reflect on the use of modern technology in relationships, in possible deceptions by your partner or in actions you might take:

1. You discover your partner has exchanged texts with a friend. The text has a sexy joke in it that you think is a bit too close for comfort. Do you:

(a) Demand that they delete the friend from the contact list, and check regularly to ensure they have not reinstated them.
(b) Ask to check the texts occasionally.
(c) Say why you feel upset about the text, and ask them not to do it again.
(d) Suggest you talk about why there was a need to exchange this kind of text.

2. You receive an e-mail from a school friend through a website that reunites school mates. They want to meet you to catch up, but you know you had a bit of a thing for each other at school and wonder if the feelings are still there. You:

(a) Decide to go, telling your partner before you set up the meeting.
(b) Ask a friend to go with you, but don't tell your partner.
(c) Ask the old school friend to come to the house to see you and your family.
(d) Ask your partner for his/her opinion about what you should do.

3. Your partner admits to receiving an e-mail from a man/woman they had a fling with some years ago. They say 'It's only an e-mail' and you let it go. Later, you discover that they have exchanged several e-mails with the same person and some contain intimate remarks. Do you:

(a) Ask your partner to stop using e-mail altogether unless you can check the messages.
(b) Say you feel betrayed and move out for a few days.
(c) Talk about why this is causing you a problem but ask your partner to let you have access to their e-mail account.
(d) Ask if there is anything in your relationship together that you both need to review.

4. Your partner goes out with a friend for a night out. When they get home you discover that they went to a lap-dancing club/male stripper evening. You:

(a) Hit the roof. They told you it would just be a night at the pub.
(b) Ban them from going to similar events in the future.
(c) Explain why you feel hurt, but rationalise it to yourself as relatively harmless.
(d) Talk together about the implications of the night out, with both of you having an equal say.

5. You discover an envelope with naked photos of a previous boy/girlfriend in your partner's bedside drawer. When you confront them, they say they like to look at them because they are artistic, but they mean nothing serious to them because they are in a relationship with you now. You:

(a) Wait until your partner has gone out and cut the pictures up before burning them.
(b) Post them back to their ex without telling your partner.
(c) Decide to accept what they have said about wanting to be with you, but privately feel hurt by their desire to keep the pictures.
(d) Explain why you feel hurt and talk through what you both want to do now.

6. Your straight partner tells you they kissed someone of the same sex in a drunken moment at a party you did not go to. You:

(a) Demand to know who it was and go round to have it out with them.
(b) Ask them to apologise to you and swear never to do it again.
(c) Try not to think about it because it was only a kiss and with someone of the same sex, which is not the same as kissing someone of the opposite sex.
(d) Talk honestly about the feelings you both have about the kiss.

7. You discover pictures of a person you do not know on your partner's mobile phone. There are messages he/she has sent saying 'miss you all the time' and 'can't wait to see you again'. Your partner says they are just a friend they met at a work event. Do you:

(a) Text the person without your partner's knowledge and tell them to back off.
(b) Tell your partner you trust them, but continue to secretly check their phone.
(c) Ask them to explain why the messages are so sexy if it is just a friend.
(d) Explain why the messages have upset you and talk through the emotions you felt when you saw the messages.

8. Your partner refuses to give you their computer password. You:

(a) Spend a lot of time when they are not around trying to guess the code.
(b) Tell him you are locking yours and make sure he knows you are e-mailing people he does not know.
(c) Try to avoid thinking about the code and tell yourself your partner needs some privacy.
(d) Ask if he/she could explain why they feel the need to password the computer in this way.

9. Your partner has a lot of friends on a social networking site and spends hours communicating with them most evenings. You are annoyed because you want to spend quality time with him/her. You:

(a) Get your own computer and spend time online yourself.
(b) Go to bed and watch television but feel disgruntled.
(c) Keep asking your partner to talk to you, even though they don't seem interested.
(d) Try to think of interesting things to do in the evening, and surprise your partner with a fun event.

10. You find a second mobile phone in your partner's coat pocket you did not know they had. You:

(a) Tell them to explain themselves and end up in a huge row about why they have this secret, during which you throw the phone at them.
(b) Ask them to show you the message box to prove their innocence.
(c) Ask for an explanation and accept their reply that they are keeping it safe for a friend.
(d) Discuss why this discovery has come as a shock to you, and look for ways of dealing with the issue.

Mostly As

You believe that any deception should not be tolerated. You are likely to get angry about secrets very quickly, and believe that your partner owes you total loyalty. You tend to see friends as possible challenges to the relationship (as well as potential affairs), and have a feeling that your partner will take a mile if given an inch. You keep them on a tight rein, and this could cause them to want to escape, leading to the very situations you fear.

If you are actually confronted by a deception, you will probably go off at the deep end, rather than look for conciliation of any kind. As far as you are concerned, e-mail, pictures and texts all constitute a threat to the relationship. For you, there is no grey area about these kinds of contact being less important than a face-to-face meeting. Your partner may well know this about you, and have accepted your viewpoint when you got together. Alternatively, they may be continually testing you to see if you will change your attitude, and this can lead to arguments. You may find yourself backed into an emotional corner if you call your partner's bluff over these kinds of deception. For example, threatening to leave if they do not let you read their text messages could find you alone and full of regret for issuing such an ultimatum.

It is important for you to think about why you feel so affected by texts, e-mail and other kinds of behaviour that your partner undertakes. Have you been hurt in the past by someone using this kind of media or doing things you feel are provocative? If you feel this way about the relationship you may have had the kind of upbringing that makes you wary of trusting other people, or feel they could easily abandon you. If you have to build your defences this high, you will have trouble keeping the relationship relaxed, pushing your partner to do the very things you are afraid of.

Mostly Bs

You blow hot and cold over your partner flirting or chatting to others using their computer or mobile phone. Some days you feel upset at their behaviour, especially if it contravenes your personal code of conduct; at other times you dismiss it as just a joke or not serious. This can give your partner confused messages about what you want, leading them to overstep the mark unintentionally. It also suggests that you have never talked together about what is appropriate in your relationship.

You are not against trying to give your partner a dose of their own medicine in order to bring them to heel, but usually find this leads to arguments and coolness in the relationship. You can sometimes keep your feelings to yourself, hoping that your partner will notice your mood and talk to you. Unfortunately, this rarely happens, and you end up disappointed. You may find yourself thinking, 'If they really loved me they would talk to me.' Of course, your partner is often oblivious to your thoughts; even if they ask you 'what's up?' you may simply say 'nothing' because you find it hard to explain exactly what you are feeling.

Strangely, you might feel a secret jealousy of some of the stuff your partner does because you would like to have the freedom to be as bold as them. It suggests that you do not have the friendships your partner has or even that you would like their sex appeal. You may have got with them partly because they took risks, and now feel uncomfortable that it is this very risk taking you find hard to manage. Your family upbringing could have been loving but a bit boring, leading you to seek out this kind of 'exciting but a bit dangerous' person once you started dating. The problem is that you are not sure how to cope with the emotions that go along with this choice. You may need to decide whether you can deal with the roller coaster of emotions on an everyday basis.

Mostly Cs

You are very accepting of your partner's behaviour, often when other people would have condemned it. There are a couple of possibilities for this – you feel very secure in the partnership or you avoid dealing with tricky situations because of the fallout that might follow if you raise the issue. You sometimes avoid even thinking about what your partner has done because it does not fit the image you have of the relationship. If you discover that your partner has been texting another man/woman, for example, you are likely to tell yourself there are lots of reasons why they are doing this, rather than jump to the conclusion that they want a relationship with them. This can be appropriate; you look for the logical reasons rather than immediately assuming the worst of your partner. However, it might also be an indicator that you are not tackling the foundation of the relationship, and fear to rock the boat just in case your partner ships out. It might be important to ask yourself if there are certain things you cannot tolerate (see the list on page 109) and raise them with your partner.

Of course, it might be that you ignore your partner's behaviour because this is how you behave, but this will only work if you both agree that your relationship is open in this way. If you expect to have this kind of openness, but want to limit your partner from behaving in the same way, you do not have a relationship of equals but one of master and slave. Your acceptance might also suggest tolerance because you want to parent your partner, and you are treating them like a naughty child rather than an adult. You are wise, though, to always ask what has actually happened rather than jumping to conclusions.

Mostly Ds

You are someone who looks for negotiated solutions to problems and hopes to find a positive way forward in the most difficult of situations. This is to your credit because difficult issues can be inflamed by a contentious approach. Looking for a way for both of you to find a way forward avoids blame, allowing you to find a neutral ground from which to move forward. However, you should be wary of crushing strong feelings about problems in order to get a solution at all costs. If you find yourself biting your tongue to avoid saying how hurt or upset you are you may feel as if you are never voicing what is really important to you. This can sometimes happen because you want the discussion to remain calm, but your strong feelings will eventually find a way out. Allow yourself to say what has caused you pain or you are likely to feel you have somehow minimised your emotions at the expense of peace.

It is also important to avoid long discussions about why the problems occurred without looking for ways to stop the difficulties in the future. Venting your mutual feelings is important. But try to agree what needs to be in place to avoid having to face this matter again in the future.

ISSUES TO DISCUSS

The new media we use raises lots of issues for couples. Some of them are just a tweak to an age-old topic – are e-mails so different to writing a letter to a lover? Others, though, can cause new problems. For example, social networking websites, such as Facebook and Friends Reunited, mean that old and new friends can be contacted at the press of a button. The speed, and often private means, of contact that this provides can cause new issues about time spent on websites and who is contacted.

Discussing the issues in the following list with your partner can help you put some ground rules in place to avoid difficulties. Work through the list separately and then come together to discuss your responses. Think about whether each issue is acceptable or unacceptable. Perhaps it is okay in some circumstances – if so, think about what these might be. You may find that you have very similar approaches to using modern media, or that you have differences in some areas.

➤ Texting other people such as friends from work without partner's knowledge.

➤ Sending cheeky/flirty/joking texts to others without partner's knowledge.

➤ Looking up old friends on Internet social networking websites.

➤ Looking up previous girl/boyfriends on websites.

➤ Looking at adult sexy images on websites.

➤ Sending adult sexy images to others.

➤ Sending pictures of yourself to others.

➤ Sending sexy pictures of yourself to others.

➤ E-mailing a stranger you met via an Internet forum or website – about a shared interest, for instance.

➤ Visiting a website you know your partner objects to.

➤ Keeping your computer or mobile phone locked at all times.

➤ Never allowing your partner to view your phone or computer.

➤ Going to lap-dancing/male stripper clubs.

➤ Indulging in 'messaging sex' with someone contacted via the Internet.

➤ Taking sexy images of each other with a camera phone.

➤ Showing sexy images of your partner to friends or colleagues.

➤ Indulging in sexy chat via forums.

➤ Watching sexy films or clips online.

➤ Leaving your details on dating websites.

Everyone has ideas about what they find acceptable and what is out of order. It is likely you will have a main list you agree on, some you are less sure about and a few on which you disagree. Think about what has motivated your response and explain it to your partner. For example, Sheila told Roger that she had decided some of the issues depended on the circumstances. This was because she found it hard to make a decision without knowing what the context might be. Roger's job was highly security conscious so keeping his computer locked was his common practice; but, as Sheila explained, it would be a different matter if his computer was not linked to work.

You may also want to reflect on whether some things would be acceptable or unacceptable if you had children who might use your computer or check out your mobile. In fact, some couples have had the cringe-making experience of their teenager reading sexy e-mails written by a parent on a computer.

Once you have looked at the list, you can trade some of your choices. So you might say, 'I don't mind you watching sexy images if you will agree to me checking out my previous boyfriend on a website.' It is also important to acknowledge that if your partner finds various activities absolutely unacceptable, and is unwilling to trade, this choice must be respected. If you do not agree, explain why, but if they feel this strongly, you will have to stand by their choice. However, if they seem to want to use the list as a way of controlling *everything* about your use of computers, mobile phones and so on, then the relationship needs to be discussed at greater length. Problems that arise out of one partner wanting the other to give up a mobile, or allow them total access to their computer, are linked to a need to keep the partner in check and have their roots in insecurity. These probably go back to attitudes learnt from their family of origin or a previous relationship where they felt out of control or even controlled by another person.

It could take some time to work your way through the list, especially if you have lots of choices that depend on circumstances. The main aim, however, is to talk about the issues raised. You may well come up with other ideas of your own; this is fine. Some of the issues may seem completely outside of your experience, while others may be familiar.

The most important questions to ask each other are 'Is this an affair?' or 'Could this be a betrayal of trust?' This is crucial because you need to agree that certain behaviours will be seen as a betrayal, rather than assume that your partner shares your views. For example, research in a relationship magazine (*Divorce Magazine*, 2009) found that men are less likely than women to regard sexual communication with another over the Internet as a form of adultery. You might, therefore, have to adjust your opinions for gender differences as well as personal taste.

Be wary of using your answers as a stick to beat your partner with in every conversation about private e-mails, mobile phone contacts or texting. You both need to recognise that answers you give are the start of a negotiation about what you can both tolerate and what would be too painful to bear. It could be useful to keep a copy of the list and check up every few months to see if your opinions change.

I think you will find that secrecy and deception cause the biggest problem in your relationship. If you agree that you can both look at sexy items on the web, for example, this defuses the difficulties that can emerge if you find one partner has deceived the other, thinking they would disapprove. Often it is not the activity that constitutes the main difficulty, but the sense that they could not share what they were doing. Having said that, finding out that your partner has registered on a dating website when you have just moved in together is never going to be a happy experience. Working through the list and sharing your feelings will be a good start in agreeing common ground.

SOME SCENARIOS

The following are all common events told to Relate counsellors. Treat them as if you are the person dealing with the dilemma. Ask yourself what you would do, and then ask your partner if you wish to. If you are reading this book without a partner, or know your partner would not take part, try to put yourself in the position of the other person to give you an all-round view. This can be an interesting approach because you might discover you feel differently about matters when forced to take another viewpoint.

1. Kerry is suspicious her partner, Alan, is seeing another woman. She secretly reads the messages on his mobile phone most evenings, looking for evidence of the affair. This goes on for three months before she eventually tells Alan she has enough material to start divorce proceedings. Should she have done this?

Is it right that Kerry secretly reads the messages? People who do this kind of relationship detective work often have suspicions about their partner long before they take action. Would it have been better to ask her partner about his behaviour much earlier, or is the material important to make sure she has evidence rather than guesswork? Ask yourself if you would do this, or how you would feel if your partner did it to you. It is possible that Kerry has wanted a divorce for a while, and the messages are a legitimate way of achieving this. Kerry may want to present the situation to friends and family as 'Alan's fault', but is this okay, even if he should not have had the affair?

2. Xavier regularly e-mails his previous girlfriend friendly information about his life and work. His wife Marie says this constitutes an affair, even though they do not meet and the e-mails are not flirty. Is she right?

The chief question here is whether Xavier should stop to please Marie, or carry on because he knows the e-mails are not about trying to restart a relationship. Marie may be jealous of the relationship that Xavier previously had with his ex-girlfriend. This could be what Marie is really feeling – a jealousy of a relationship that she had no part in. Some couples agree to cut contact with previous lovers, while others are happy to tolerate friendships with ex-partners. Which camp do you fall into? If Xavier met his ex regularly at the pub, would this be different to the e-mails? If so, why? How would Marie feel if Xavier agreed to stop, but secretly e-mailed his ex from the computer at work? The boundary with friendships and ex-partners can be difficult to negotiate, but you may discover you have different ideas about where the boundary lies.

3. Max tells his wife Gina to change her mobile number after he finds suggestive texts from a work colleague on her phone. He says he cannot trust her until she does this. Is he right to demand this?

If you found suggestive texts on your partner's phone, would you think it was their fault for allowing them, or the fault of the person who sent them? In essence, this is the problem for

Gina and Max. Max has made the assumption that Gina wanted or solicited the texts, but she may be as upset as Max about the situation. In fact, she could be suffering harassment from the work colleague. Do you think Gina is having an affair? If so, what evidence is there for this? If you found this kind of text, would you jump to the conclusion that infidelity had occurred or think it was a mistake of some kind? How you feel about this kind of thing could give you some important indicators about the strength of the communication in your relationship.

4. *Jan finds an adult pornographic website on the site history of her computer. It is not an illegal site, but does contain graphic pictures of naked women. She confronts Barry who tells her to stop making a fuss and that it is 'no big deal'. Jan is upset at Barry's attitude, as well as the fact that he used her computer rather than his to look at the site. She withdraws from him, sleeping in the spare room for several weeks. Should she have reacted as she did?*

The key part of this dilemma is how Jan (and you) regard pornography. I am not talking about illegal porn, which is not tolerable to the majority of people, but the kind of site that shows consenting adults in sexual poses. Many people use porn in their daily life; semi-pornographic images can be found in advertising, and frank shows about sexual technique are featured on late-night mainstream television. Porn is not the secretive activity it used to be but couples often have ambivalent feelings about its use. Both sexes can find that the perfect (often digitally altered) images make them feel inferior or that their lovemaking techniques are not as adventurous.

Jan and Barry may have opposing views of porn that they have never discussed. Why did Barry use Jan's computer? Was he making a point, or provoking Jan to get a reaction? The issue about using your partner's computer or phone can bring to the surface concerns around privacy and secrecy that many couples have never discussed, although previous generations had similar problems with locked desks or secret boxes under the bed. By sleeping separately, Jan is trying to tell Barry very clearly that his behaviour is not acceptable. She is also being a bit manipulative – see things my way or no way. It could be that Barry has met this kind of behaviour before from Jan over other issues in the relationship, and that viewing the porn is a way of telling her that he is capable of making his own decisions. It's a powerful way of doing this, but perhaps this is what it takes to get Jan to listen to him.

5. Sam discovers that Natasha has been on a website forum for people talking about meeting new partners. She has used it to talk exclusively to a man, and has told him that her sex life with Sam is 'dull'. She has not talked to Sam about this, and as far as he is concerned, their sex life is good. They have a big row, and Natasha threatens to leave him. When things calm down, Sam asks Natasha to use her laptop only when he is in the room. Should he ask this? Is there any harm in Natasha talking to a stranger in this way?

Why did Natasha make the comments she did to the stranger on the forum? This is probably the key issue here and involves some guesswork about Natasha's motivation. It's possible that Natasha finds it difficult to talk to Sam about sex, but the anonymity of the Internet allowed her to be more open. Or she may secretly have wanted Sam to find out what she said and realise that she was unhappy without having to deal with telling him face to face. Natasha seems to feel freer telling things to the people in the forum, and this may suggest she feels constrained in some way at home.

Have you had this experience – that it is easier to put things in an e-mail or message to strangers than talk to your family? Many people report this phenomenon. This may be because you can avoid interruptions or silences by using e-mail. In addition, you can compose an e-mail in a way you cannot control a conversation. You can frame the exact words you want to use – even be insulting or angry – without fear of the recipient leaving the room or swearing at you. Sometimes the writing of the e-mail is the release the person needs. They may not care if the other person responds or not, although often it is hoped that the message will have got through loud and clear.

Sam's request that Natasha uses the computer only with him is also challenging. Would you want this? If so, why? Sam seems to want control, but none of this addresses the chief problem – that Natasha seems to want a change to their sex life.

All these dilemmas are the kind of thing that Relate counsellors hear in their consulting rooms across the UK every day. The problem for most people is that each situation is unique to them. Finding a way forward can be difficult, especially when what was once a simple matter of learning that your partner has had a face-to-face affair is now a complex web of levels of deception, some of which your partner may not even regard as a threat to your relationship.

Deciding what to do as a consequence of working all this out can be even more fraught with problems. In a Relate survey on affairs, about 31 per cent of respondents who had experienced an affair found it resulted in a permanent breakdown of the relationship. However, about 22 per cent thought the affair was positive, bringing problems out into the open. So is there anything to be learnt from the use of modern technology that could benefit your committed relationship?

WHY DO PEOPLE USE TEXTS AND E-MAILS IN AFFAIRS?

It might seem an odd question to ask, but it bears some analysis and could help you understand why you might have used texts and/or e-mails to flirt or connect with someone instead of arranging to meet face-to-face (although you might do this too).

1. YOU CAN BE WHO YOU WANT TO BE

Even if you know the person you are flirting with in another context (perhaps at work or via a friend), using texts and e-mails can unleash a hidden side of you. You may be shy, but given the time to compose a text with exactly the words you want to use, you can sound like the most romantic or suggestive person they have ever met. No more stumbling over the feelings you are trying to express or watching while someone else says what you want to say. You might be more open and direct about what you like sexually, or phrase a sexy remark in a style you think suits the mood of the person you want to impress.

This phenomenon of the 'e-mail alter ego' is well known, and can lead to people sending inappropriate messages because their braver side is let out of the cage. For example, a woman lost her job after e-mailing her boss several choice messages about what she saw as her bullying in the workplace. She could not bring herself to speak in person, but managed to be very blunt in the e-mail.

This behaviour has pluses and minuses. On the minus side, you may find a mild flirtation takes on a life of its own, causing you to feel you must follow through, perhaps having a full-on affair you never intended. On the plus side, you could discover a more confident side to yourself that you can utilise in everyday life. The trick is to understand how to integrate the side of yourself you find in the e-mails to your best advantage. You can use this in a committed relationship to improve closeness and connection.

2. THE THRILL OF DECEPTION

The intoxication of deception is a big part of affairs. Often, once the affair is revealed, the excitement and passion die away very quickly. This is because naughtiness adds an adrenaline kick that is not unlike dangerous sports – affairs can have the same physiological effect as riding on a roller coaster. Secretly texting your lover while your partner is sitting in the next room can speed your heartbeat, quicken your breathing and give you butterflies in your stomach. This can help to affirm that the affair is special and worth doing, although these feelings are often short lived and spurious. You might feel that the affair is meeting your need for excitement that is missing in your usual partnership. Years ago, this thrill would have been possible only in secret telephone calls, and before that, in clandestine letters. Texts and e-mails are speedier, available at any time and can be answered in a flash, upping the thrill factor with each reply.

If you have embarked on an affair as an act of revenge against your partner, seeing them squirm when your phone beeps with a new message – especially if you lie about who has messaged you – can feel like getting your own back. Their discomfiture can allow you a feeling of victory. Some people deliberately leave their phones lying around or a computer unlocked so that their partner will read the messages from a lover just to achieve this painful experience and hurt them in a way they may have been hurt. This method of dealing with your problems is never to be recommended – see Chapter 9 to find a way of talking about your difficulties.

3. IT FEELS LIKE INTIMACY

Exchanging lots of texts or other messages with a secret lover can seem like getting really close to them. It's possible to send hundreds of messages in a day, but the truth is that this is 'intimacy lite'. Most of what you send will be of the 'what you doing?' variety, and will lack the complexity of looking at your lover and reading their body language (this is true even if you have a webcam). To get to know someone you need to spend lots of time with them in person, learning who they are, what they want from life and, in the case of sexual contact, what turns them on.

If you struggle to maintain committed relationships with long-term partners, texting a lover can feel as if you are engaged in a deeper relationship than you have previously had. This can lead you to feel you are not failing at achieving closeness – especially if your committed partner has accused you of being unable to be emotionally intimate – and bolster your emotional esteem.

4. BECAUSE IT'S EASY

A simple reason, but a very common explanation. If you had to go to a lot of trouble to make contact with the person you fancied you would probably never embark on the affair in the first place. Leaving the house on a cold winter's evening to find a working public phone to call someone you hope is at home could cool the ardour of the hottest lover. Texting and e-mailing are so easy and extremely tempting. To use an analogy, the reason we are all getting fatter is because we no longer have to spend hours each day preparing and cooking our food. Instead, we can buy a ready meal or takeaway with very little thought about cooking it. Text love is like this. We can send a message with not much thought about the impact on the receiver and respond speedily to their message to us. Texting can also have an addictive quality, leading individuals to carry on writing to each other even when the original reason for doing so has waned. Many a person having an affair has been found out by their partner reading a phone bill pages long with lists of texts, sometimes amounting to hundreds of pounds.

5. YOU CAN CONTROL THE SEX

This may not seem an obvious reason for using text – surely the object of an affair is to have wild uncontrollable sex? The truth is, though, that affairs are often about control. The illicit relationship has to be kept to certain times and locations; the sex has to be managed so that the partner does not notice anything strange – no love bites or unusual perfume – and hidden from family and friends. Instead of a raging passion, it therefore has to fit carefully into set parameters.

Text sex is another manifestation of this phenomenon. If you send sexually explicit texts to each other, perhaps while you are both masturbating, then you are in charge. You can have, or not have, an orgasm. You can lie to the other person about how aroused you are and whether you have enjoyed the text exchange. Phone sex is more or less the same, and again puts you in charge of the experience. Face-to-face sex is rarely this controllable. It's true that some sex games are based on controlling the other, but essentially you have to negotiate what you are doing. This is not true for sex exchanged on modern media.

For some people, this degree of control is stress relieving and unthreatening. They do not have to risk the vulnerability of making a mistake during lovemaking, or worrying that the text partner is scrutinising their body. It can appeal to people who have been hurt in a relationship, or who want to remain in control of their responses to a given situation. Or it may simply be that the feeling of control allows the text affair to keep within certain limits, avoiding the reality of a committed sexual relationship.

CAN PORNOGRAPHY BE AN 'AFFAIR'?

The viewing of pornography has grown enormously in the last 20 years. Once, anyone who wanted to view pornography bought under-the-counter magazines or went to see 'naturist' films in grotty private cinemas. Of course, prostitution is as old as civilisation, and strippers were dancing for payment hundreds of years ago. Victorian gents (the richer ones) often had secret collections of nude paintings and photos – Prince Albert had a nude painting of a woman in his bathroom that he and Victoria were said to enjoy. Most of these pictures would be viewed as innocent by today's standards, although some of the paintings on the ancient walls of Pompeii leave little to the imagination. Modern pornography, though, is not like this. If you want to find images and videos of virtually any sexual preference, you have only to surf the net for a few minutes.

So is it possible for someone to initiate 'affair'-type behaviour with a set of images on the net? To answer this question it is important to assess what the impact of porn on a relationship might be. Here is the story of one couple who encountered a problem with porn in their partnership:

Sadie and Liam, both aged 40, have been married for 14 years and have two daughters, aged 10 and 7. Their sex life has not been so great since their younger daughter was born, but they care for one another and accept this as an inevitable part of a busy family life. Liam spends a lot of time using his computer because he works from home as a design consultant, while Sadie is a classroom assistant at her local school.

Liam often looks at porn while the family is out of the house, finding it exciting and soothing. He likes pictures of women with large breasts and has accumulated hundreds of these images in a file he has locked with a password. He tends to organise them into categories such as hair colour, breast size or ethnicity, and, dependent on his mood, has particular times when he looks at certain kinds of women in his collection.

Gradually, he spends more and more of his day surfing, collecting and looking at these pictures and videos. Although he finds them sexually exciting, he does not always use them for masturbation, although this is part of his viewing activity; he mainly enjoys the sense of control he has over his collection, and the secret thrill that Sadie does not know about 'his women'. He also spends a lot of money on the porn, but hides this from Sadie by using a secret credit card.

Liam's work starts to suffer, and Sadie realises that they are getting into debt. Several of Liam's employers stop using him because he does not meet deadlines or seem interested in the commissions they offer. Sadie is confused – Liam seems to be on the computer at all hours, but there is no work coming in or being done. She is also hurt that Liam is withdrawn and less and less concerned about the family, spending little time with the girls, even at weekends. Eventually, Sadie loses her temper with Liam and accuses him of having no interest in her. She threatens to leave him and even goes as far as to start packing. Liam breaks down, and in a terrible evening that drags on into the night, admits his activities.

Sadie is astounded, with no idea that this is what Liam has been doing. She demands to see the images, and Liam shows her what he has. Sadie is devastated. She feels inadequate and unattractive when she looks at the women in the pictures, wonders if Liam still cares for her and eventually becomes angry that they are in debt and in danger of losing everything because of Liam's behaviour. Liam promises never to look at the porn again, but Sadie cannot believe he will keep his promise and wonders if she can ever trust him again. They try to sleep, but in the morning face an uphill

*struggle to rebuild their relationship. Sadie says that they
must go to Relate as a condition of them staying together.*

As you read about Sadie and Liam you could probably see the
similarities between Liam's behaviour and the affairs already
described in this book. Here are some of the reasons that
people who have partners who use porn describe it as like an
affair:

It Distracts the User From Their Family/Partner

All affairs distract the person having them from their committed relationship or family. Sometimes this happens because
the person having the affair feels uncared for or unhappy in the
partnership and looks for solace elsewhere. It can also be a side
issue to the main reason the affair has occurred. Using porn is
like this. Viewing porn has an addictive quality. This is not
because it is so sexually arousing that the person keeps
returning, but because the desire to add one more image to a
collection grips the frequent user. The strong pull of the
computer can cause an emotional cut-off from everyday life. If
you have ever experienced the excitement of new love, you
know how all-absorbing it can be. Affairs cause this effect
because the attention of the individual pursuing the affair is
concentrated on the person they are pursuing – and porn usage
can be the same.

When Discovered, It Can Cause Jealousy and Anxiety

If your partner is discovered using porn they may say, 'It's only
pictures, not real people. I haven't picked someone up in a bar.'
This reasoning can feel like a hollow consolation. More men
than women use porn in a systematic way (although women
view porn more than they did 10 years ago) so the typical
scenario is that the female partner discovers her male partner
viewing young women. As with Sadie in the case study above,

she may look at the women in the images and feel she can never hope to live up to the way they look.

In addition, many of the pornographic images and videos show women enjoying sexual activities that the man's partner may not want to carry out. The most common issues that women state are not okay for them are some sexual positions, anal or oral sex, swinging or group sex, or sex that edges into violence from the partner. Such activities often feature in pornographic images on the net. Experts sometimes describe this as 'normalising' sexual practices, making them seem acceptable in everyday relationships, when in fact they are often unusual sexual behaviours enjoyed by a small percentage of the population.

The female partner may therefore be hit by a double whammy – feeling inadequate or unattractive to her partner and that she is a sexual prude because she does not want to do what the people on the video are doing. Saying she is put off by the activities shown can leave her open to remarks from her partner along the lines of, 'It's just normal sex; it wouldn't be on here if it wasn't.' So all the feelings generated by an affair are present in the viewing of porn – feelings of inadequacy, fear about the future and some sense of betrayal, even though the people in the pictures are not real in the relationship. In fact, the sense of betrayal of a partner secretly using porn can be greater than finding out they have had an affair with a real person because there is no other to deal with or speak to; just a set of unknown people in anonymous pictures.

It is also important to note that most pornographic images are digitally altered in post-production, and this is now even possible in videos. So if you feel diminished by the body shape of the person in the porn it is because you are dealing with images that are not real in the first place. This probably will not make much difference in the immediate aftermath of the discovery of the porn, but it is worth remembering if you find yourself in this position.

It Destroys Trust

Secret viewing of porn, and then the revelation of this, is nearly always accompanied by the destruction of trust. If your partner has told you they are spending a long time on the computer for work, or has hidden their viewing on an unknown mobile phone, you could be forgiven for wondering if you can trust them in the future. As with 'real' affairs, you may also wonder if you can trust your judgment in the future. Your immediate instinct could be to take the computer away or cut up the SIM card but this is dealing with the symptoms instead of the cause of the breakdown in trust.

For frequent users, porn can act as a 'self-soothing' mechanism – that is, it calms the user down, diminishing anxiety. The problem is that this is often short lived and, like some other external 'soothers' (alcohol, gambling and so on), can also escalate. So, if looking at porn once a week is calming, it will gradually lose its effect, leading to daily viewing or more. Of course, not everyone who views porn will head down this path, in the same way that not everyone who enjoys a glass of wine becomes an alcoholic. However, using porn to deal with stress and anxiety can lead to this problem because the need for greater input is driven by increasing stress, creating a vicious circle of need and porn viewing. It also has some of the same attraction of alcohol or drugs in that it is intermittently rewarding. This just means that not every image will be arousing, so a search has to be made for the 'right' image causing, at its worst, hours of net surfing.

Some people feel that they must not disturb the person using porn in case the stress worsens. They may therefore try to hide their feelings, brushing the discovery under the carpet. The embarrassment factor of porn use, and the reluctance of either of you to talk to others about it, can lead to a pretence that nothing has really happened. You may be willing to tell a close friend your partner has had an affair with someone from work, but less keen to admit they have spent hundreds of pounds looking at pornographic pictures on the net.

It Prevents You From Having a Satisfying Sexual Relationship

If you stay with your partner after an affair is revealed, sex is one of the last things to eventually resume. You may experience the phenomenon of having lots of sex when you first decide to stay together, but this can be a passing event, part of the process of trying to bond with each other again. It might also be a way of saying, 'See, I am as sexy as your lover, and just as willing to do the things they did with you.' Eventually, though, you will have to sort out what you want from your sex life in the long run.

This experience is not unusual after the discovery of extensive porn use. You may feel you have something to prove, that 'real' sex is better than screen sex. Alternatively, you may want to retreat, sleeping separately and avoiding affection or sexual initiatives from your partner. Conversely, they may seek more touching and sexual contact to reassure them that the relationship is still as it has always been, or to allay guilt. If you withdraw while they try to get closer, neither of you will feel satisfied, leading to arguments and feelings of anxiety.

If you have seen the images that your partner looked at, you may experience flashes of these during lovemaking. This can be upsetting and disruptive to enjoying sex, especially if you are in the fragile phase of starting again after the discovery of your partner's behaviour. This also happens after a one-to-one affair is discovered, but the 'images' are imagined or built up from things you may know about the lover. The pictures or videos you may have looked at, perhaps to understand why your partner viewed them, will be more graphic and impactful. Unfortunately, people who become addicted to porn can often experience problems in making love to a real person because the images are available on tap and do not demand commitment or personal responsibility. Ultimately, this can cause great hurt in the relationship.

You Fear the Temptation Will Always Be There

As with affairs with other people, the fear that your partner will return to using porn may be present long after the discovery of this activity. If your partner had an affair with someone in a nearby town, you could ask them never to go there again as you repair your partnership, but this cannot be said of the computer or mobile phone. You could destroy any porn DVDs but the computer is now seen as a family necessity. Making a partner promise never to use the computer in this way again is not likely to give you the result you want because all the promises your partner makes can be open to your own doubts.

WHAT TO DO WHEN YOU DISCOVER YOUR PARTNER USES PORN

You may struggle to understand why they wanted to use porn, especially if you thought your sex life was okay. It is important to remember that porn use is not chiefly about sexual expression, but often about stress release and self-comforting. This is not an easy concept to grasp, but if you can understand why the porn was used in the first place you stand a real chance of diminishing or stopping it rather than it continuing to be a problem you cannot solve.

Try to Understand the Reasons Why Your Partner Uses Porn

You may not feel very sympathetic to your partner if you are hurt and angry because of their clandestine porn use, but stress and anxiety are likely to be the underlying reasons. They may not even realise that this is the deeper reason for their behaviour, but in counselling this is nearly always what emerges. Sometimes the anxiety is the legacy of an unhappy childhood, and is a chronic condition that your partner has not recognised. In other situations the stress is due to work or family worries. These may be solvable in a shorter period of time. Try using relaxation methods such as relaxation CDs (widely available), yoga, regular exercise and making full use of days off. A technique called 'mindfulness' has also been found to be extremely helpful to obsessive thinking, compulsive behaviour and depression. This is now available through practising therapists (look on the British Association for Counselling and Psychotherapy website for therapists who list it) or your GP may be able to recommend a practitioner locally who can help you learn the technique. You could also read *Full Catastrophe Living* by Jon Kabat-Zinn for more information on this technique.

Use Practical Action to Diminish the Likelihood of Porn Viewing

You can take some simple steps to help overcome the chances of the computer being used secretly again. If the PC or laptop has been used in a room away from other people, reposition it so those using it are in general view. Create a small computer area where all the family can use it when they need to. Agree that the laptop is only used in family rooms. Set up blocks to certain websites in the way that families often do for young children.

Agree with your partner that you will view their surfing history periodically. Be wary, though, of being cast as their 'policeman' as this can lead to arguments and a lack of trust because you may find yourself thinking they are incapable of monitoring their own use. If your partner has tended to sit up late in the evening after you have gone to bed, or stayed at home when you and the family have gone out, agree to the same bedtime and that both of you will go on trips out.

Destroy saved files and DVDs featuring porn, making sure that computer files are truly deleted rather than retrievable in some other way. The person who viewed the porn should do this with their partner. If you are the partner, avoid taking on this task as you may be viewed with private resentment by your partner, even if they appeared to agree to the process. Although you may find it difficult, let your partner know you understand this is hard for them and that you want to support them.

Talk About the Effect On Your Relationship

Pushing the revelation of porn viewing under the carpet means you are likely to have to deal with it in the future. If you are the person who discovered your partner has viewed porn, you need to express how you feel. You may be very angry, and it is important that you have an outlet for this (without physical aggression), but if you simply have a huge row and then act as if nothing has happened, nothing will be resolved. Explain how you feel about the discovery and ask your partner why they have used the porn. Tell your partner if you find yourself wondering about the future of the relationship, and what you think will have to happen to resolve the situation. As in all types of affairs, do not make snap decisions about what you want to do. Even if you suspect that viewing the porn spells the end of the relationship, try to discuss this when you feel calmer and more able to think through the options open to both of you.

Do not tell children what you have discovered, especially if they are too young to understand the complications of the situation. It is not unusual for an angry partner to spill secrets to children in order to punish the partner they see as guilty, but this can be as much of a punishment for the child as the adult. If they witness you arguing, reassure them that you will sort out the issue and that they are not to blame for any of the problems.

Consider attending couple counselling at Relate to help you talk through the implications of your use of porn and the discovery of the secret. If you fear that a counsellor will be embarrassed to hear about porn, do not worry. Relate counsellors are trained to work with issues around sexuality, with porn use being one. Also, an experienced counsellor will have heard many similar stories over the years and will understand about the effect on the two of you.

Ask Yourself If This Could Be Sexual Addiction

If you fear that the porn viewing is linked to other behaviours you are uncomfortable about, and you have met this problem repeatedly in the relationship, you may be dealing with addictive behaviour. If compulsive masturbation and the need to view porn interferes with work and family life to such a degree that your partner has repeatedly lost jobs or previous partners, then the problem may be more serious than it first appears. Seek help from your GP or specialist therapists who deal with sexual addiction. Websites such as www.sexual-addiction.co.uk (specialist therapists) and www.slaauk.org (similar to AA for alcoholics) could offer information to help you decide what you want to do if you recognise this problem in your partner or yourself.

This chapter has dealt with many different forms of modern media and how they can affect couples in ways similar to more traditional affairs. The answer to the question posed by the title 'Is this an affair?' is probably yes. If the online flirtation, exchange of texts or viewing of sexy images online causes problems with trust, makes arguments worse and diminishes your sense of self-worth when you discover it, then it has virtually the same emotional impact as a face-to-face affair. You will need to take the same steps outlined in other parts of this book to recover and decide whether the relationship has a future.

CHAPTER 5

What Triggers an Affair?

Affairs, online or face-to-face, do not just appear out of the blue. In most cases, there are events that lead to their appearance. Many couples do not always recognise these events. Indeed, they may consider that the event or set of circumstances is irrelevant. This can develop a sort of 'relationship blindness' that prevents the couple taking action on their feelings long before an affair looms on the horizon. Sometimes the relationship blindness comes from fear. The couple may be afraid to voice anxiety about a specific issue – such as a sexual or financial problem – or decide that it will resolve itself without intervention from either partner. Here are some common triggers to affairs.

A FAMILY BEREAVEMENT

If you have experienced a death in the family you will know that the effects of bereavement can be long lasting. People may say and do things that are out of character or find that the death is a powerful reminder of their own mortality. If a relationship is already experiencing some stresses and strains, these feelings may take over. For instance, one partner may decide that they should find a way out of an unhappy relationship before their life is also over, embarking on a 'door opener' affair (see page 70). They could begin an 'experimental' affair (see page 88) to see if they want an alternative lifestyle to the one they have chosen. Sometimes the affair that follows bereavement is linked to a desire to seek the warmth and reassurance that is not supplied by the person's committed relationship. This is the equivalent of blindly reaching out for support in order to climb out of a dark pit, and seizing the first hand that is offered.

If the partner who does not have the affair is the person who has been bereaved they may appear so wrapped up in their grief that their partner seeks attention from another. This is often an intense friendship rather than a full-blown sexual affair, but it can cause extra unhappiness to a partner already coping with the loss of a loved one. Shock and sadness after a death can cause some people to take actions they later regret. Even if this appears to be the case, examination of the relationship may point out problems that existed before the affair.

Ways to Prevent This Kind of Affair

Make sure you talk about the impact of the death. If your partner (or you) is finding it hard to discuss the loss, it can help to let them know you are available when they feel ready to talk. Just say something like, 'I am here when you need me. Let me know if I can help with anything, or you would just like to talk.' Offer physical warmth and affection. A cuddle or loving word can help your partner to know you care when words are hard to say. Keep this up for a long time after the death, as bereavement is not quickly dealt with.

If you have suffered bereavement and have found it has had an unexpectedly negative impact on you, tell your partner how you are feeling. Ask for support in a clear way. For example, avoid saying, 'You never give me a hug these days.' Instead, try, 'I feel really miserable. I could do with a hug.'

If you realise that the death has caused you to reassess your own life in some way, share this with your partner. If you bottle it up you may come to resent your partner because they have not instinctively realised the way in which the death has affected you. Talking about the effect on your own life can help you both to face the coming years in a more understanding way.

REACHING MID-LIFE

The mid-life crisis is something of a cliché these days, but there is some evidence that people do experience changes around mid-life. Studies suggest that women use the time in their mid-40s to reflect on their life in the past, assess how they are living in the present and make plans for the future. It seems reasonable to assume that men may go through the same kind of life assessment as women, but without the hormonal changes that women experience. The result of these reflections can be that they want to throw off some of the old ways of living and experience new ones. An affair is often a symbol of wanting this new lifestyle. The desire to cast off an old life for a new one may be a sudden desire or the culmination of a growing discomfort over many years.

Ways to Prevent This Kind of Affair

Prepare for mid-life by spending some time talking about your hopes and expectations for the future. Avoid making assumptions about your partner staying the same person forever, and be ready to face the challenge of change.

When you reach your mid-40s give your relationship a 'health check'. Ask yourself and your partner what you think of the relationship and what you want from the future. Take action on dreams and long-held hopes. For example, if one of you has always wanted to go to Florida, list all the things you would have to do to make it happen. Then tackle the list!

Watch out for warning signs that mid-life storms are brewing. Dissatisfaction with a job that was previously acceptable, arguments with teenage children (especially of the same sex as the parent), changes in style of dress and a desire to socialise in old haunts may indicate that a mid-life crisis is under way. Talk about the signs, and ask what they mean to the partner displaying them.

MONEY WORRIES

According to a survey by Relate, money is the number one topic that couples argue about. Money problems can lead to a desire for an affair as an escape route from the tension the couple is experiencing. Interestingly, arguments about money may develop because the two people in the partnership put their head in the sand, hoping that the problem will go away. When the opportunity for an affair comes along it adds to this self-deception, soon causing the couple to face a multi-layered mess of deception and avoidance. The affair may start out feeling like a break from reality but it can soon become a prison of lies and deceit that causes the couple to break up.

Ways to Prevent This Kind of Affair

Keep a close eye on your money! This means talking about how you will deal with the financial side of your life from the moment you become a couple. Decide basic things such as who will pay bills and manage the accounts or credit cards, and what amount of cash you think each of you should spend each week.

Get advice as soon as things begin to look wobbly. Putting a large bill away in a drawer is no way to manage your accounts and you could end up with huge rows about whose fault it is. It is precisely this situation that can lead to the temptation to have an affair, because your partner may begin to seem like a nag or a miser. Call advice lines for gas and electricity payments and credit card helplines if you run into debt, or use websites that offer reputable cash advice. You can often be helped to pay off your debts without running into further trouble.

Think about what money represents in your partnership. Does it feel as if one person holds the purse strings and consequently all the power? Are you ducking the reality of your financial situation because it seems unromantic to talk about money? Are you both anxious to hang on to your own cash? Do you want to maintain your individuality in case you are hurt by putting too much of yourself into an uncertain relationship? Once you have analysed the feelings behind the cash, you will be better placed to sort out any underlying problems.

A KEY LIFESTYLE CHANGE

Affairs can follow a key lifestyle change such as moving house, losing or gaining a job and recovering from an illness – in fact, almost anything that has put you under some form of stress. Even good things, such as achieving promotion at work, can be stressful because you will be expected to meet the challenges of the new job. You may be tempted to seek an affair because you are trying to find your feet in a new and strange situation. This can lead you to abandon the normal supports you would rely on – your partner, family and friends – to find new ways to get you through.

An affair may seem attractive because the person you choose to have the affair with does not know your usual coping strategies and may be able to help you deal with the strange situation. For example, you may embark on an affair with a person at your new place of work because they understand the firm and the situation you are in. The same may be said of affairs that take place with new neighbours, health care workers who have got you through an illness or anyone who offers understanding about your new environment.

Ways to Prevent This Kind of Affair

You first need to consider why an affair suddenly seems attractive at this point in your life. Try to assess if you feel emotionally vulnerable and, if so, why. For example, now that you have moved to a bigger house, are you worried about paying the extra mortgage? Have you and your partner discussed the change and thought through the implications of moving house? Do you miss friends and neighbours from your old home? This technique of asking yourself why you feel the way you do is a useful skill that can help you in many different situations. It is especially helpful if you are wondering about an affair because it can buy you 'thinking time' to assess the implications of your actions.

Talk to your partner about your feelings connected to the lifestyle change. Express any uncertainties you may feel about the future or the excitement you may be experiencing at the prospect of your new role. Ask them for their feelings about your situation, as they are likely to be involved in any change you have made.

RELATIONSHIP PROBLEMS

This really covers all the problems that people may find in relationships, from frequent bitter arguments to parenting problems and sexual difficulties. The chief reason that an affair may seem attractive in these circumstances is perhaps obvious: it appears to be an escape – a safe haven – from the problems in the relationship. As you have read, this is often illusory and unlikely to solve the relationship problems in the long run.

Ways to Prevent This Kind of Affair

Maintain effective communication. Talk to each other about your pleasures and problems. Listen to your partner without jumping in to have your say. Make your feelings clear. For example, avoid saying, 'You don't care about me any more.' Instead, say what has made you feel uncared for. You might feel uncared for because they never bring you a morning cup of tea, seem uninterested in your work or refuse to help bath the baby when you are tired. If you are specific you may find that things change. Being unclear in your communication can mean you never achieve what you really want.

Be aware of the 'crunch points' that couples often encounter. Problem areas can be:

➤ settling in together

➤ the birth of the first child

➤ difficulties in achieving a balance between home and work life

➤ dealing with your growing family

➤ caring for parents or other family members

➤ when children leave home

➤ spending more time together when work ends

Discuss these key points and think about how you will cope with them ahead of time, rather than waiting to discover the pitfalls when you are in the middle of them.

Discuss sexual concerns early in your relationship. You may feel embarrassed or uncertain, but if you can develop a sexual 'language' it will stand you in good stead for the future. Even if you have not done this in the past, it is never too late to start. Remember that sexual desire ebbs and flows according to the state of your partnership and any external pressures on the two of you. For instance, feeling tired, stressed or anxious about your children can dampen down your sex drive. Relaxing, having fun and laughing together can all boost your sexual desire and are worth cultivating.

All affairs have similarities and so do their causes. In general, they come from a desire to find a simple way of coping with a complex situation in the committed relationship. Some represent a desire to escape, return a hurt given by a partner, explore a new way of relating or avoid being vulnerable with a partner. The problem is that there rarely are simple ways of solving a problem that has been built up over several years in a committed relationship. Affairs are not solutions, however tempting it may be to regard them in this light. They always add complications to an already tricky situation and have the potential to hurt a family or a partner a great deal. In the next chapter we will explore the feelings and outcomes of affairs, including the emotions of the people in the affair triangle.

CHAPTER 6

What Really Happens
in an Affair?

In earlier chapters we explored the reasons why affairs occur and considered the role of trust in relationships. This chapter will look at the feelings, emotions and behaviour that you may encounter when an affair starts. The emotions involved in affairs can seem like a roller coaster ride – one moment sublime and exciting, the next full of guilt and confusion. Some people seem to enjoy the drama of these sorts of encounters, relishing the highs and lows. For most people, though, the experience of an affair can be difficult to manage – even if the affair eventually leads to a committed relationship. Most of these feelings come from the very nature of affairs. Usually they remain a secret (at least for a while) and represent the breaking of a trust. In modern society these are taboo areas that people strive to avoid.

Imagine that you are told on a Monday that a work colleague is going to be sacked on the Friday. You are asked to keep this a secret. You meet the colleague in the staff room, and they talk to you about their hopes for their future career in the firm. All the time you want to tell them that they are about to lose the job they have such high hopes for, but know you cannot do this. Instead, you smile and perhaps lie, all the while trying to cut the conversation short. At the end of the week, you meet your colleague clearing their desk. They angrily accuse you of being 'a liar' and 'thoughtless'. You feel awful and wish you could have done something helpful. The tension you felt during the awkward conversation in the staff room is how many people feel during an affair, whether they are the person having the affair, the lover or the partner of the person in the affair. You may feel on edge and tense, and may perhaps develop physical symptoms of anxiety such as headaches and stomach problems, followed by a desire to avoid the situation. Alongside this, you could experience the euphoria of strong feelings for another person.

All this can lead to a great deal of emotional confusion. It is no wonder that many people feel in a mess during an affair! They are usually coping with a huge variety of emotions that often appear to make no sense at all. All this confusion can make the simplest decision problematic or painful. You may feel torn about telling your partner or keeping the affair secret. If you are a friend, you may struggle with yourself about telling others about the affair you have discovered. If you are the lover, you may long to be with the person you are having the affair with, but afraid of the consequences.

COMMON FEELINGS WHEN STARTING AN AFFAIR

DESIRE

This is perhaps the overwhelming emotion experienced at the start of an affair. Often it feels like the powerful emotions that usually accompany new relationships. The person you want to have the affair with seems wonderful – the most attractive, most fun and most exciting person you have met. You may make comparisons with your present partner, seeing in the person you want the affair with all the attributes your partner lacks. Your strong desire may be linked to sexual feelings, but it could just as easily be the feeling that you have found a 'soul mate' or a very close friendship.

EXCITEMENT AND PLEASURE

Sometimes a partner says in counselling, 'I don't know why he/she had the affair.' The answer is simple at an emotional level. Affairs are pleasurable and exciting and usually offer something to the person that they lack elsewhere. Otherwise, there would be no point in starting an affair. Although the reasons for an affair are many and complex, the actual gut feelings at the beginning are often very good. The excitement and pleasure in an affair can also be heightened by the 'naughtiness factor'. The knowledge that what you are doing is wrong can add a *frisson* of enjoyment that gives the affair greater sexual arousal and pleasure than an open relationship can provide.

UNCERTAINTY

Many people are very uncertain at the start of an affair. They may feel torn in two about their actions and fearful of being found out. It is also possible for you to begin an affair feeling pushed along by events, only later realising the uncertainty of your feelings about what you have done. For instance, John realised three weeks into a steamy liaison with his wife's friend that he had embarked on a relationship he had not planned or thought through. In the early stages, the combination of sexual desire and hyped-up excitement robs you of clear thinking about your actions.

DEFENSIVENESS

As the affair proceeds you may find yourself justifying it. You may tell yourself that 'if my husband or wife took more notice of me, I wouldn't need to do this' or 'it's only for a short while', or even the good old cliché, 'they mean nothing to me'. This last defensive remark is similar to the smoker who says, 'Sure, I smoke 20 a day, but I can give up whenever I like.' In other words, your conscience is feeling under pressure and you are attempting to find a way of allowing the affair to continue without facing the inevitable decision about what happens next. Your partner may notice this defensiveness as you snap their head off over a simple matter. For example, Lisa jumped on her husband's remark when he wondered why she had started to walk to work rather than use the bus. Lisa snappily replied it was none of his business. She was meeting her lover on the way to work, and felt pressurised by her husband's observation.

RELIEF

This may seem an unexpected feeling during an affair, but it is one that many people describe. The relief can be connected to a feeling that they are still attractive or able to function sexually, and it is not unusual in couples with a severe sexual problem. For example, if a man suffers from impotence and embarks on an affair, he experiences a feeling of relief if he is able to maintain an erection with his lover.

An affair that happens because of a relationship that has been in trouble may seem like a harbour in a storm. For example, Louisa had been married to Mark for seven years when she met Sam. Mark had been violent towards Louisa during the latter part of their marriage; Sam offered Louisa all that she lacked, chiefly understanding and care. She did not leave Mark immediately as they had a five-year-old daughter and Louisa was concerned about taking the child away from her father. She saw Sam for several months before leaving Mark a note telling him she was leaving him. During the months before the end of the marriage, Louisa experienced great feelings of relief that there was someone she could turn to who understood and loved her.

SELF-ABSORPTION

Many affairs have the effect of creating 'emotional blinkers'. You may feel as if the affair is unconnected to any other part of your life. Some people describe this as the 'box effect' – the affair is like a box that is opened when the lovers meet. This can mean that the needs of your family and friends recede into the background so that you become totally absorbed in the affair and what is going on in that part of your life alone.

It is not unusual for people who are having an affair to lie about it and to believe they are not lying. They actually come to believe the lies they are telling to cover up the affair because they see them as justifiable in the circumstances. Eventually the 'box effect' can cause the person to weave a very complicated web of deceit indeed in order to keep the affair and the other parts of their life apart.

ANXIETY

At the beginning of an affair you may feel euphoric and excited. Eventually, though, you will come down from this high. It is at this stage that you may begin to feel anxious. The struggle to maintain the secret of the affair may feel like a heavier and heavier burden as time passes. Even if the actual affair ends swiftly, anxiety about being found out may dog you for months or years. Anxiety can be physical – a churning stomach, headaches and muscle tension are all common if a person feels under stress or anxious. The accumulation of anxiety is often the reason that people tell their partner about the affair. They simply cannot bear to carry the feelings any longer and blurt them out to their unsuspecting partner.

INCREASED SEXUAL DESIRE

If the affair is sexual, you may find that the sex you experience has all the novelty of sex with a new partner. It may feel exciting and passionate, perhaps reflecting everything you have lost in your current relationship. Part of the attraction of most affairs is the desire to make love with your new lover, but something strange also happens – some people report an increased desire to make love to their committed partner as well. This may seem puzzling, but if your libido is boosted it may mean that you want sex more often and turn to your committed partner as well as your lover.

Another explanation is that, like the 'three-legged stool' affair (see page 73), the affair relieves the pressure on your committed relationship, creating room for sexual desire and affection to return. This can often cause great pain to your partner once the affair is revealed. They will feel betrayed, and sometimes physically repulsed, by the knowledge that you slept with your lover and them at the same time.

If you have crushed sexual desire for some time, perhaps because your partner has lost interest in sex, you may feel set free by the affair and allow yourself to pursue unusual sexual outlets. This can be dangerous because you may not follow 'safe sex' procedures and run the risk of pregnancy or of catching a sexually transmitted infection. Some men who seek sex outside of their committed relationships may see a prostitute. Although not strictly an affair in the usual sense, when the committed partner finds out about the prostitute they are usually devastated: they may feel as if they are completely worthless if their partner prefers a prostitute to them. Recovery from this experience can take a long time and may require a great deal of hard work if the relationship is to survive.

DENIAL

Strangely, at the beginning of an affair, many people deny to themselves that they are having an affair. They may blank out their committed partner (even if they see them every day) and instead concentrate totally on the time they have with their lover. This is not intentional, but probably a psychological defence against the guilt that they know is lurking under the surface.

Affairs also escalate from small beginnings, unless you find yourself in a drunken one-night stand. An exchange of texts with someone you met at a conference moves to phone calls taken when your partner is not around, through to agreements to meet and then to creating times when you can have sex together. All this takes time – sometimes weeks or months – so a degree of self-deception can creep in.

Denying to yourself that you intend to have an affair, or are actually having one, may seem strange, but this process happens in other parts of life. Imagine you are on a diet. You know you should not eat the chocolate you bought your child, but somehow it calls to you. When they are at school you find yourself in the kitchen, eating the chocolate. Later, you cannot remember how you decided to go to the kitchen or look in the cupboard; you only know you ate it. We deny to ourselves our actions all the time, but with affairs the denial can last a long time. Some people say that when the affair is found out they feel as though they have woken up and realised the events were real and now they have to face the music with their partner. So denial can act like soundproofing, preventing you from 'hearing' the consequences of your actions.

THE AFFAIR TRIANGLE

All affairs are triangular. They involve three people who are trying to manage a relationship. One person is trying to manage two relationships: that is the person who has the affair. One person – the committed partner – is trying to be in a relationship with the partner who is having the affair. The third person is the lover who is having a relationship with the other partner. This triangle can only be sustained as long as these three people remain in it. If one partner says they wish to leave, or the affair is revealed and the committed partner wants out, the triangle is dissolved.

For an affair to last, the triangle has to survive. This is perhaps obvious, but it is not always completely understood by people who embark on an affair. They may entertain fantasies about maintaining two relationships with ease or moving from one relationship to another without disturbance to their committed partner. This rarely happens. Once an affair is revealed and accepted as truth by all the parties it will have a cataclysmic effect on their relationship and lifestyle. I have added 'accepted as truth' as the committed partner often denies the truth of what is happening, even if the evidence is unambiguous.

> *Anya and Bill had been married for five years when Bill had an affair with Sarah. They met at a social event held by the factory where Bill worked and were soon meeting several times a week. A close friend of Bill's decided that Bill was acting irresponsibly and told Anya what was happening. The friend was astounded when Anya refused point-blank to accept what he was saying. She said she trusted Bill and that his evenings out were spent with friends building a stock car for racing. The friend then told Anya he would take her to the pub that Sarah and Bill went to, but Anya still refused. In fact, the affair went on for over a year before Anya was willing to admit that there could be a problem. Anya could not admit the possibility of an affair because she was afraid. Fear often prevents people from tackling a difficult issue, and Anya was like this.*

The following table illustrates the common responses of all three people involved in the triangle of an affair. This can also help to explain the different impacts of affairs that are short or long lived.

	The person having the affair	The partner of the person having the affair	The lover
Stage 1 – At the beginning			
	Justification – 'I need this affair because things are so bad with my partner.'	Concern – 'There are problems in our relationship, but I don't know how/am too afraid to tackle them.'	Desire – 'I want a relationship with this person. It's up to them if they tell their partner.'
	Desire – 'I really want to be with this person.'	Denial – 'Perhaps things will work out on their own.'	Pleasure – 'This affair is exciting.'
Stage 2 – As the affair progresses			
	Denial – 'This affair is making no difference to my committed relationship.'	Questioning – 'My partner seems different, but I don't know why.'	Questioning – 'I wonder where this affair is heading. What does he/she mean to me?'
Stage 3 – If the affair continues			
	Questioning – 'I am not sure where the affair is going. Is it more important to me than my committed relationship?'	Anxiety – 'My partner is behaving very differently and is often secretive. I wonder if they are seeing someone else?'	Seeking answers – 'I want to know what we are doing. I will ask them if they want an ongoing relationship.'
Stage 4 – If the affair is revealed			
	Confusion – 'I thought I could contain the affair. Now it is out of control. I feel guilty about the situation.'	Unhappiness – 'I thought I knew my partner, but they are like a stranger to me. I feel betrayed.'	Uncertainty – 'I don't know what is going to happen now. Will our relationship continue? Do I want it to?'
Stage 5 – After the affair			
	Unhappiness – 'I don't know what I want. Should I stay in my committed relationship?'	Confusion – 'I don't know what I want to happen. Should our relationship continue?'	Uncertainty – 'I wonder whether we still have a relationship. Should I wait to find out or finish it now? I feel used and angry.'

Short-term Affairs

One-night stands, or affairs that last a few weeks, may only register the feelings described in Stage 1, although they can have the same effect for the partner of the person who has the affair as described in Stages 4 and 5. As the table suggests, the lover and the person having the affair are less likely to feel involved with each other and therefore to register the affair as a threat to the committed relationship.

This can explain why people who have 'flings' do not see them as likely to upset their committed partner, while their partner feels extremely upset and let down. This can result in communication reaching an all-time low as the partner who has been betrayed struggles to convince their partner that there has been a serious negative effect on the relationship. This is the kind of affair that people often describe as 'just sex' or 'they meant nothing to me'. What it means to the person who has the affair can be very different to what it means to their partner.

This is a crucial point for most affairs. It is not what happens in the affair – sexual or non-sexual, long or short – but the 'fallout' effect on the committed partnership. It is not possible to create an emotional chart that says 'all short-term affairs are harmless' or 'all long-term affairs will end a committed relationship'. Each affair is unique and will be handled differently by the three people in the triangle, although there are some responses that are common to most affairs.

Long-term Affairs

Longer-term affairs, that last a few months or more, are likely to arouse the feelings described at Stages 2 and 3. These affairs are often characterised by denial and the 'blinkered emotions' described earlier. People caught in this type of affair are likely to be in a transitional stage – the relationship is not yet sufficiently mature to warrant making decisions about the future but has had enough of an impact to cause the person to think about what will happen to their committed relationship. As the table indicates, denial of the reality of the affair is common. The lover is less likely to deny the significance, but may want to play along with the idea that the affair is 'harmless'.

Long-term affairs that last months or years will move through all the stages described in the table. Denial, and then a pressing need to face the reality of what has happened, can dim initial excitement. There will be a significant investment by the person having the affair and their lover in each other, which means that revealing it is bound to have a strong effect on the committed relationship. This type of affair is also often a 'three-legged stool' affair, so that it may even have steadied the committed relationship. Revealing it may cause a tidal wave of emotion that can threaten to engulf the three people in the triangle. However, this is not an excuse to avoid talking about the affair. The vast majority of affairs are a smokescreen for problems in the committed relationship, and it is these that need attention. It is possible that the committed relationship will end as a consequence of the affair, but perhaps this is kinder than three people living their lives full of uncertainty and built on lies.

LOOKING AT ALL SIDES OF THE TRIANGLE

Each person in the triangle will have different feelings about the affair, depending on their viewpoint. How they feel will affect their behaviour and the decisions they make. Here are some different views of the same affair from the three people involved in it. As you read the case study, try to imagine yourself as one of the characters and think about how you would have behaved in the same situation.

Erica and Martin have been living together for several years. They are teachers in different schools, but have no children of their own. Erica had to have a serious gynaecological operation two years ago. It has taken her a long time to recover, and their sex life has taken a backward step during this time. Added to this, Martin has been feeling insecure at his school as the board of governors is considering cutting the staff. They both work long hours and are often tired when they are together.

Erica is just beginning to wonder if their partnership can survive when she meets Tim. Tim is the single parent of Ian, one of her pupils, and they are instantly attracted, although Erica holds back from voicing her feelings. Then Tim helps out on a school trip with Erica and they spend most of the time talking together about work and other shared interests. At the end of the day, Erica agrees to meet Tim for a walk and their affair begins.

Tim has been lonely since his divorce. He sees Erica as a person he can talk to, and finds her very attractive. He is unsure about how Martin would react if he found out about the affair, but somehow feels comforted by the fact that Erica and Martin are not married. He finds himself thinking that Erica is 'fair game' and that it is up to her to tell him if they go too far. Erica and Tim enjoy their sex life, which seems lighter and more joyful than Erica's sexual experiences with Martin.

After six months, Erica decides that she must tell Martin about Tim. She chooses a quiet evening together and tells Martin that she is having an affair. At first, Martin does not believe what Erica is saying but after a while he realises that she is serious. He begins to cry and Erica feels dreadful. She had begun to tell herself that Martin might be relieved that their partnership was over. Instead, Erica finds herself wondering if she has done the right thing, and how she is going to choose between Martin and Tim.

If all three people in this triangle had kept a journal during this time, it might have looked like this:

Erica's Journal

Met Tim at school today. He is really good-looking and I know I am attracted to him, but I must keep a lid on my feelings. What would Martin say?

Spent the day with Tim on a school trip. I know it is wrong, but I really fancy him. Our arms brushed on the coach and it felt like an electric shock. I am sure he fancies me too. He has asked me if I would like to walk by the river tomorrow and we agreed to meet at 7pm. I don't know if I will turn up. I will have to find an excuse to tell Martin.

Met Tim and have now seen him five times in the last month. We made love for the first time last night — it was great! Today I feel mixed up — guilty and happy at the same time. Perhaps I can keep this from Martin. After all, I don't know what is going to happen next. It might all end soon. There is no point in telling Martin if that's the case. It will only hurt him unnecessarily.

Tim and I are getting more serious, and I feel completely confused. I feel worse than ever about keeping all this secret. Every time I see Tim I feel excited but also a sense of dread. It's just so difficult to know where I am headed. I never thought I would end up in such a difficult situation.

I've decided. I must tell Martin about Tim. I can't go on living a lie like this. Tim isn't keen on this idea. He thinks that telling Martin will end everything. He doesn't understand why we can't go on as we are. It's all right for him; he hasn't got a partner to worry about.

I've told Martin. It's awful. He is really upset and keeps begging me to give Tim up. I don't know how I am going to decide what to do, especially as Tim has never suggested making a permanent relationship. Perhaps I've done the wrong thing. I don't know what is going to happen next.

Martin's Journal

Things have been very difficult at work lately. I don't know if I am handling the kids well and I am expecting to be made redundant at any moment. Erica and I are not getting on, especially in bed. Our love life has never recovered since her op, and I feel so tired all the time.

Erica seems to be in a better mood lately. She is happier and easier to talk to. Perhaps things are improving for us. I am afraid to talk about the difficulties we have experienced lately in case talking just makes things worse.

Erica is putting in a lot of evening work at school. She hardly seems to be in the house at all. I've also caught her out telling the odd lie about where she's been and I am beginning to wonder what is going on. Could she be seeing someone else? I really hope I'm imagining things because I couldn't take it if she is having an affair. My confidence is at rock bottom already.

Erica is definitely lying. She told me she had to visit her sister, but her sister called while she was out and she wasn't there. Where is she? The worry is killing me. What am I going to do?

Erica has told me she is having an affair with a man called Tim. I feel completely gutted. I just want her to stay. I feel sick, angry and broken. I can't believe she did this to me.

Tim's Journal

I met Erica today. She is a teacher at Ian's school. I think she is gorgeous. I asked one of the other parents if she is married and she said no, but she thought she has a boyfriend.

Erica and I spent all day together today. I know she fancies me — I can just feel it when we look at each other. I've asked her to meet me at the park. I really hope she turns up.

We did meet and she does have a boyfriend. In fact, she lives with a man called Martin but they're not married. I think that means she's up for it. After all, if they were serious they would have got married by now. Erica says that it's not like that, but I think differently. I want her and I'm going to try to get her.

We made love last night. It was everything I hoped for. Erica is lovely and I really think I might be falling in love with her, but I don't know if I am ready to make a commitment because of Ian. I wouldn't want Ian to be hurt again in the way he was after his mother and I divorced. Perhaps Erica and I could just see each other for a while until I feel more certain.

Erica keeps talking about Martin. If she tells him now it will provoke a difficult situation because he will probably give Erica an ultimatum — stay and give me up, or go with me. I'm not ready for that. I want her to wait, but she says she feels guilty at all the deception. Well, so do I, but we will be far more ready to be together if she only hangs on for a bit longer.

Erica has told Martin. She came here in floods of tears saying he has taken it very badly and she doesn't know which way to turn. I feel confused and fed up. Now I don't know what is going to happen.

Most people in an affair triangle experience the transfer of emotions that Erica, Tim and Martin describe. Once uncertainty or anxiety affects one person, it can move round the triangle easily, often preventing the three people involved from seeing things in a clear way. This is why affairs can be so painful – you may not only be going through your own sadness or confusion, but also picking up two other people's feelings as well.

UNDERSTANDING WHAT HAPPENED IN YOUR AFFAIR

If you have found yourself in an affair triangle it is useful to try to make sense of what actually happened. Earlier in the book you read about the different types of affair, and have perhaps discovered if your experience fits into one of these categories. Now use the following questionnaires to examine what is happening (or has happened) to you and why. The first questionnaire is relevant if you have had an affair. The second is for people who have discovered that their partner has been unfaithful.

Many people do not fully understand why they acted the way they did during an affair. Completing this questionnaire will help you to understand any feelings you have experienced.

1. When the affair first began, my overriding feeling was one of:

(a) Guilt and fear that it would be found out.
(b) Euphoria and excitement.
(c) Uncertainty that it was the right thing to do.

2. Once the affair was underway, it felt as if:

(a) It would be hard for me/us to handle if it lasted more than a few weeks.
(b) It could easily be kept a secret.
(c) The tension of the uncertainty made the affair less enjoyable than it had been at the start.

3. As the affair continued it felt:

(a) As if it was getting out of control.
(b) Less exciting than at the start.
(c) As if something would cause it to snap – that we could easily break up.

4. Deciding what to do about the affair became:

(a) Confusing – our emotions were pulled in lots of different directions.
(b) More and more difficult to talk about.
(c) Too hard to discuss because we argued about the future.

5. When/if the affair was revealed:

(a) I felt relieved that my committed partner knew about it.
(b) It was the end of the affair because we couldn't cope with the fallout.
(c) It was very difficult to know if we had done the right thing in revealing the affair.

Mostly As

As the person who had the affair, you always felt guilty. Your answers reveal that you probably wanted your partner to find out about the affair all along because the stress of maintaining the deception was so pressurising. It is possible you began the affair thinking it would be short-lived, or perhaps had a one-night stand rather than a long-term commitment. If the affair has finished you may look back on it as a mistake and wish it had never happened. Your guilty feelings could indicate that, at base, you have a commitment to your partner that was not completely broken by the affair. You would benefit from looking at the reasons why the affair started (see Chapter 3) as there may be unresolved issues in your committed relationship.

Mostly Bs

As the person who had the affair, you probably entered this affair in a light-hearted way, possibly seeing it as a 'bit of fun' that could not really harm the committed relationship in the triangle. As the affair continued, though, it became clear that it was becoming much more than either of you were prepared for. Instead of growing into a relationship that had the potential for a future of some sort, it became increasingly difficult to make sense of. Your communication may have ground to a halt, suggesting that the affair was based on sexual attraction alone or that neither of you ever intended it to be more than a diversion from your committed relationships. When the affair was revealed the pain it caused the third party in the triangle may have taken you by surprise. This is because neither of you took it seriously and perhaps came to believe that if *you* did not think it was serious then neither would the other partner. This kind of affair is often opportunistic and you may be the sort of person who tends to seize the moment rather than consider your actions in depth.

Mostly Cs

As the person who had the affair, it seems as if you entered this affair very tentatively. From the outset one, or both, of you felt unsure that having the affair was wise, but found yourselves having a relationship nevertheless. You may have felt as if you were on an 'emotional autopilot', seeing each other but experiencing very mixed feelings. You could also have felt that the affair was meeting a deep need in you, fearing that ending it would deny you the means to have your need met. This kind of response often occurs in a sexless affair where a close friendship develops, rather than a passionate exchange. Your uncertainty about revealing the affair might come from a feeling that you are not actually doing 'something wrong' rather than a desire to hide it from a partner. Unlike some other kinds of affair, the revelation of this type is not experienced (partly) as a relief, but only serves to create further feelings of confusion and anxiety. You need to untangle the deeper reasons for your affair and then take stock of what you want for the future.

If you are the committed partner of someone who had an affair, answer the following questions to discover why you behaved the way you did:

1. When I first suspected the affair I:

(a) Thought I must be mistaken.
(b) Recognised the signs from previous affairs.
(c) Felt extremely anxious.

2. As time went by and my suspicions grew I:

(a) Tried to tell myself it was not true.
(b) Felt more and more sure that an affair was happening.
(c) Felt afraid to tackle my partner.

3. During this time I noticed that my partner:

(a) Became withdrawn but I put it down to overwork or other stress.
(b) Became more affectionate. This was a repeating pattern from other affairs.
(c) Made some attempts to talk to me, but I was too scared and avoided listening to them.

4. When I found out about the affair I:

(a) Was shocked and disbelieving.
(b) Was upset but not surprised.
(c) Tried to avoid dealing with the affair.

5. Looking back, I wish I had:

(a) Taken notice of the signs of the affair.
(b) Tackled my partner much more quickly.
(c) Been braver in dealing with the affair.

Mostly As

You were probably deeply shocked by what was happening and sought to protect yourself by avoiding the truth. You may have found yourself making excuses for your partner and seeking to protect them if others told you they were having an affair. At a deeper level, you may have realised that there were important reasons why the affair happened – perhaps trouble in the family or other strains had contributed to your partner's desire to escape. In the aftermath, it is likely that you have struggled to make sense of what happened and still feel upset by the affair.

Mostly Bs

You have experienced your partner's affairs before and recognised the signs with some degree of cynicism. You may have decided to stay together for a variety of reasons – maybe children, finances or fear of being alone – but feel that the relationship will never be a trusting one if the affairs continue. You have built a high defensive wall around yourself that protects you from the sadness and pain of your situation, but probably also means that you are cut off from enjoying a loving relationship. You may wish that you could change things but feel you lack the resources to do this.

Mostly Cs

You have been in denial about the affair and sought to avoid even thinking about what was happening. As a result you feel emotionally handcuffed – unable to cope with what has happened because you cannot even admit it to yourself. You may never be able to deal fully with the situation, sweeping it under the carpet in order to avoid thinking about why and how it happened. You could run the danger of seeing your partner have repeated affairs because the crucial reasons about why the affair happened have not been resolved.

The chapters so far have aimed to help you make sense of affairs and why they happen. The next section will deal with the aftermath of an affair – how it can be revealed, the effect on all three people involved and the fallout among their friends and family. It will help you to learn more about common reactions to affairs and what you can do to move forward once the affair has been revealed.

PART III

RECOVERING FROM
BROKEN TRUST

CHAPTER 7

Finding Out About the Affair

The revelation of an affair is one of the most difficult and traumatic experiences that a couple can go through. Even if you have had suspicions about an affair, or wanted to tell your partner that you are involved in an affair, it can still be extremely difficult to weather the emotional storms that usually follow when all three people in the triangle know that the affair has been discovered.

Most affairs are not revealed in the dramatic way that characters in soap operas tend to go in for. For the ordinary couple, the discovery or telling of an affair usually takes place in the most mundane situations – sitting at the dining room table, in bed, or even with friends. Sometimes the affair is discovered by the committed partner when they are alone, and sometimes when they are with their partner or others. However people learn about it, it can still be a painful and miserable experience.

WAYS TO FIND OUT ABOUT AN AFFAIR

Here are some of the common ways that you might learn about an affair.

FINDING CLUES

It is not unusual for one member of a couple to tell me in counselling that they became aware of an affair by discovering 'clues' left by their partner. Clues can take a wide variety of forms, such as tickets for events and receipts for meals that you know nothing about. Searching through a partner's text messages in their phone or finding recently visited websites on the computer are increasingly common methods of discovery. You might notice locked drawers that have never been locked before; some condoms in a pocket or car glove compartment; or e-mails and cards from the lover. Sometimes you may actually have been searching for these kinds of clue because you think your partner is having an affair, or have stumbled across them while putting the washing in the machine or looking for cash in a handbag.

Although it may seem surprising, your unfaithful partner may have left these clues deliberately. I do not mean that they have planted them in order to let you know what is happening (although I have met people who have done this). Rather, they want the affair to be revealed, perhaps unconsciously, but are afraid to tell their partner outright. Leaving clues that are likely to be found is a way of putting the responsibility for talking about the affair into the hands of the partner who makes the discovery. In general, this is not a helpful way to reveal or discover an affair. In effect, the person having the affair abdicates responsibility, passing it to the person who is probably least equipped to cope – the partner who has not had the affair. This can lead to a communication block at the very time when you need to talk to each other.

If you have not been expecting to find clues to an affair, you are likely to feel shock, including the physical experience of shock. You could feel dizzy or sick when you first realise you are holding a picture text message from a lover to your partner. If the clues are less well defined – such as a credit card slip for an unfamiliar restaurant – you may search your mind for a simple explanation. Seeking to explain away such clues is very understandable because of the long-term implications of an affair. You may find that your mind races between wanting to believe that you have made a mistake and feeling sure that an affair has really happened. You may want to tackle your partner immediately, or sit on your feelings for days. All of these reactions are completely normal.

YOU ARE TOLD ABOUT THE AFFAIR BY OTHERS

Of all the ways in which you might learn about an affair, this is probably the most embarrassing. A friend might tell you because they have discovered the affair and feel it is right to tell you. If they are the only other person who knows, you may feel less awkward than if you are the last to know, when everyone else you work or socialise with has realised long ago. Perhaps worse is the public outing of an affair on a social networking site.

People usually tell someone whose partner is having an affair out of good intentions – perhaps because they put themselves in the shoes of the partner who is being deceived. Your mind will probably be in turmoil when you hear the news and you may feel obliged to explain away your partner's behaviour while you struggle to believe what you have heard. Sometimes you may not hear the news in a direct way. The person telling you may leave an anonymous phone message, send an e-mail or write a text. Although supposedly helpful, this can leave you plenty of room to dismiss the message or letter as 'a mistake', or to worry about it while you try to think about how to talk to your partner. Occasionally, this kind of anonymous contact is vindictive and can be sent by someone who harbours a grudge against you or your partner. No affair may have taken place, but the experience might leave you both disturbed and anxious about what has happened.

As with other forms of discovery, you are likely to feel shocked by hearing about an affair in this way. You may also find yourself trying to keep a mask of normality while feeling as if you are falling apart inside. If you discover that a number of other people knew about the affair while you were still in the dark you will probably feel embarrassed and uncertain about how to discuss the situation. You could find yourself wondering who to trust if your workmates, relatives or friends have kept such a secret from you. You may want to ask your partner about the truth of the rumour straight away, or undertake your own investigations with others first. You may be tempted to contact mutual friends to find out if they know about the affair, or just to see if they will tell you what has been going on. Alternatively, you may cut yourself off from others because you cannot face the fact that they knew about the affair long before you.

YOU ARE TOLD ABOUT THE AFFAIR BY THE LOVER

Hearing about the affair from your partner's lover can be hard to handle. They may approach you in person or contact you by phone, text or e-mail. If they arrive at your door and tell you that they are the person your partner is having an affair with, your first thoughts may be that they are lying. Alternatively, you may experience a feeling that people some-times tell me is rather like 'finding a missing jigsaw piece'. This feeling can be so strong that they describe meeting the lover as 'a kind of relief'. However, even if their arrival helps to make clear some unexplained events in your relationship over the last few months or longer, the meeting is likely to be emo-tionally charged. Some of what happens will be dependent on the way the lover presents himself or herself. For instance, they may be angry, despairing or afraid. You could be faced with dealing with someone who is extremely emotional, as well as your own feelings.

Learning about an affair via a letter or text from a partner's lover is also very difficult, although you will at least have extra time to think through how you might approach your partner. You could deny to yourself that the letter is real or true while awaiting more information from your partner.

Whether the lover tells you the news in person or through a message, your immediate feeling is likely to be surprise and unhappiness. You may break down in tears, feel aggressive towards the lover or feel distant, as if the events are happening to someone else. You could also experience an unexpected empathy with the lover, feeling that you have both been ill-used by your partner, especially if the lover has only just discovered that the person they thought was theirs alone is actually married to or living with you. This can explain why some people develop an alliance with their partner's lover.

Alternatively, you could feel as if the lover is to blame for all your relationship troubles and want to attack them, verbally or physically. Confronted with the reality of the lover in person, you are less able to hide behind the idea that the affair is not true or find an excuse to describe it as a mistake. This can mean that meeting the lover feels as if a hammer has smashed your life apart. These are normal feelings, but can be very hard to deal with.

YOU ARE TOLD ABOUT THE AFFAIR BY YOUR PARTNER

This may be the most straightforward way to learn about the affair, but it is probably also the most difficult to handle. If your partner tells you in a thoughtful way, perhaps after explaining that they want to talk to you about something important and putting time aside to tell you about the affair, you are likely to be upset and perhaps angry, but less able to hide behind a defensive feeling that the affair is not real. If your partner blurts out the affair in the middle of a row, you may feel as if the ground has opened up beneath you. Either way, you will experience the full emotional reality of the affair and this can be very difficult to cope with. Some couples I have counselled describe it as being like an 'emotional steamroller', almost literally taking their breath away. Even if you had suspected for some time that the affair was going on, you may wonder what the future holds now that it is out in the open.

Your response to hearing from a partner about an affair will be coloured by the way in which you are told. If you have some time to ask questions and express *your* feelings, you will cope better than if your partner tells you about the affair and then storms out of the room. Whatever your deeper feelings about the affair, however, in the first few days after learning about it you will experience a powerful mixture of emotions – anger and sadness, shock and resignation. If your partner stays with you, it is likely that you will want answers to your questions and also time alone. You might even push your partner away if they try to apologise, or become so angry that you throw things around. All of this is normal, but if there is any violence that threatens you or your partner you must take appropriate steps to protect yourself. Do not stay and hope the violence will not escalate.

RESPONDING TO THE REVELATION

How you respond to the revelation of an affair can depend on how you have dealt with difficult events in the past. Most couples have a pattern of response that they tend to follow once something uncomfortable has emerged in the relationship. Read the following descriptions to determine which of these most closely follows your own method of talking about or dealing with a tricky issue. Each description is followed by suggestions on how to manage finding out about an affair within your usual style.

THE VOLCANIC EXPLOSION (VE) COUPLE

As a couple you are likely to handle difficult situations by venting your feelings in a noisy and expressive manner. You may scream and shout at each other or have several bitter arguments, one after the other. You may have long periods between these emotional eruptions, even reacting calmly when you experience minor irritations in life. Every so often, though, you will have a huge explosion of anger and vitriol when every problem you have encountered is brought to the surface and argued about. Sometimes these arguments can be sparked by a seemingly unrelated issue, but once started, every slight either one of you has ever felt is dragged into the row. Afterwards, you may feel exhausted and spend time apart to 'lick your wounds'.

The relationship may then resume relatively quietly, although you may not have resolved the problems you fought over. For example, Jay and Freya could argue for the Olympics. Their friends often teased them about their fiery rows, but to Jay and Freya, they were not funny. On one occasion, Jay became so angry he punched a hole in their lounge door. As usual, their argument was over a trivial issue – whose turn it was to stack the dishwasher – but their inability to calm things down caused an episode that frightened them both. They avoided talking to each other about anything other than the basics of living together for weeks for fear of anything else happening.

The Volcanic Explosion Couple and Affairs

As you can imagine, the revelation of an affair for the VE couple can be terrifying to behold. The couple is likely to argue so fiercely that they may themselves feel frightened of the emotions they have unleashed. There is also a real risk of violence, so it is better to try to keep things as calm as possible. The VE couple should avoid admitting an affair in the context of an argument, instead telling their partner in as calm a manner as possible. If things appear to be getting overheated, they should call 'time out', deciding to continue talking later or even the next day. This method does require discipline, but can help the VE couple to keep reasonably calm. It is important, however, to add that angry feelings are a natural result of hearing about an affair, so they do need to be vented. The anger should help to lead to a more productive discussion about what has happened, rather than shutting the door to further talking.

In general, the VE couple has explosive rows (about affairs or any pertinent issue) because they tend to crush their irritation rather than allowing it to escape. They are like a saucepan that eventually boils over so VE couples need to lift the lid occasionally to reduce the heat. Sharing feelings of disappointment or annoyance at the time when they occur can be less destructive than blowing up every six weeks, with little communication afterwards, perhaps for several weeks.

THE CIRCULAR ROW (CR) COUPLE

Couples who row repeatedly over the same kinds of issue can be described as the 'circular row' couple. This is because their arguments simply go round and round the same circle of problems. They hardly ever resolve problems, usually finding that these return in some other form.

For instance, Vera and Winston regularly argue over Vera's gifts to her daughter by her first marriage. Winston feels they are unnecessary, whereas Vera thinks they help to support her daughter, who is raising two children alone. Vera and Winston have never arrived at a conclusion to their rows, or even found a practical way of sorting the problems out – such as fixing a cash limit on the gifts. Instead, each time Vera goes shopping, Winston inspects her bags and demands to know what she has bought. If this issue goes cold, Vera may accuse Winston of spending too much time at the pub or spending their savings on gambling on horse racing. Money is clearly a big issue for Winston and Vera, but they never sort out the real problem, which is probably connected to how much they are committed to each other, mixed with a little jealousy of the people and things the other gives time to.

This kind of circular arguing can be emotionally exhausting, not to say pointless. Both partners may long for a break from the bickering, but feel unsure of how to change. Sometimes it can feel as if each partner engages in the arguing because it is a familiar routine rather than as an effort to voice concerns.

The Circular Row Couple and Affairs

Couples who indulge in circular rows may find that trying to talk about an affair is not only painful but also hard work. A particular issue – such as the sexual side of the affair – may become their chief focus, and their rows are likely to centre on this. Discussions and arguments may get tangled up on such issues, with the couple behaving like a dog with a bone, continually tugging their differing points of view back and forth. The partner who has not had the affair may want to ask the same or linked questions over and over, with the partner who had the affair feeling under attack and unable to answer the questions in a way that appears to satisfy their partner. There may be periods of intense discussion followed by periods of relative quiet, but the CR couple will not have resolved their issues: they will be waiting to resurrect them for the next bout of arguing.

Because of the habit-forming nature of circular rows, breaking the cycle of the CR couple can be tough, but not impossible. When discussing the affair the couple may need to agree a contract that allows them to ask questions on particular concerns at a certain time. For instance, Alastair and James agreed that they would only discuss Alastair's infidelity in the evenings between six and seven o'clock. At other times, they concentrated on rebuilding and improving their relationship in other ways. They talked through the changes they wanted to make that would help them to be closer, thereby preventing the reasons that the infidelity occurred in the first place.

A need to take practical action can be important for the CR couple. Circular arguments are often maintained because the couple feel frozen into reacting to their partner rather than acting to effect change. For example, Siobhan and Max decided to move house so that Max would avoid seeing a neighbour with whom he had had a one-night stand. This helped them to feel they had made a new start in their marriage, and was a powerful symbol to Siobhan that Max was really committed to her.

THE PUSH PROBLEMS UNDER THE CARPET (PPC) COUPLE

The 'push problems under the carpet' couple tend to deal with difficult issues by avoiding discussing problems at all. As soon as a particular concern emerges the couple may simply stop talking to each other or switch to another issue. Usually this is because of fear about the impact of the problem, or an anxiety that they will not be able to sort out the issue. Most people put difficult issues to the back of their mind for a short period sometimes. In fact this can be beneficial, as it allows the unconscious to work on the issue before the problem receives conscious attention. If, though, the problem is never brought into the light of day it can fester away, gradually eating away at the relationship until it falters. Eventually, if enough difficulties are pushed under the carpet, the couple falls over the enormous hill of concerns lying in the middle of their relationship!

For example, Marie and Jeff found talking about their daughter extremely difficult. Jeff thought that Marie asked too much of their daughter, Suzanne, expecting her to read well and always to come top of her class even though she was only eight. Marie thought that Jeff was undemanding of Suzanne and did not properly encourage her schoolwork. After a number of skirmishes, they avoided the subject completely, hardly ever discussing Suzanne's progress at school. As a result, Suzanne felt torn about how to behave at school and suffered a real dilemma about which parent to please. Her schoolwork began to suffer, with the result that Marie and Jeff were called to the school to discuss the difficulties that Suzanne had encountered.

One of the chief problems for the PPC couple is that because they never discuss troublesome issues, they never develop the skills they need to talk about problems. The whole scenario then becomes self-perpetuating. In the end, the lack of practice – and the already attendant fear of analysing the situation – means that the couple are stuck in an emotional no man's land, unable to move forward or backward to resolve the issues they need to address.

The Push Problems Under the Carpet Couple and Affairs

As you might expect, the PPC couple can struggle to make sense of what has happened to them after an affair. Not only is it very difficult for the couple to talk about it, but the silence between them could also lead them to make unrealistic assumptions about the aftermath of the affair.

For example, Peter and Natalie had been through an unhappy time after Natalie's affair. They had been made very miserable when Natalie's boyfriend, David, had told Peter about the affair. Although the revelation of the affair also ended the relationship between Natalie and David, neither Natalie nor Peter knew how to talk about what had happened. After a few months of silence, Peter told himself that Natalie must have made a commitment to their relationship because she had stayed with him rather than going to be with David. This, however, was far from the truth. Natalie felt extremely ambivalent about remaining in the marriage. She had initially remained with Peter because she knew in her heart that she did not love David enough to move in with him. She also felt very unsure about her feelings towards Peter, and began to make plans to move out in order to give herself some 'mental space' to think things over. One day, Peter came home to find a note on the kitchen table from Natalie telling him that she had left him. Peter was devastated by Natalie's actions and found it very hard to recover from her departure.

PPC couples can counteract their inclination to push tricky issues aside by creating a checklist of questions that they ask each other when they realise this is happening. The list can help because it can provide a catalyst to action.

The following are some suggestions for such a list. Most of the questions are 'open questions' – that is, they require more detailed answers than just a yes or no. An example of a 'closed question' is 'Do you like that picture?' It would be hard to answer anything but yes or no to such an enquiry. An example of an open question might be 'What do you think about that picture?' This allows plenty of room for the person replying to say what they like or dislike about the picture. This technique is important for PPC couples as they often employ closed questions rather than open ones.

➤ How do you feel about (concern – such as an affair)?

➤ What do you think we should do about (concern)?

➤ Why did you say what you did about the (concern)?

➤ What steps do you think we should take to sort (concern) out?

➤ Why do you think the (concern) happened?

Most open questions ask the partner for their opinion or feelings about an issue. The reason that PPC couples avoid using them is precisely because they are afraid to hear exactly what their partner does feel. Overcoming this fear is important because fear can lock up conversations at the very time when it is vital to talk about what has happened.

TALKING ABOUT THE AFFAIR

Even if you are the most tolerant and understanding person, talking about an affair can be incredibly difficult. Swirling around your discussions are likely to be some extremely messy emotions. Guilt, anger, sadness and the desire for revenge can all spill out once an infidelity has been revealed. Although all these emotions are natural, they can prevent you from talking and listening to each other. This can, in turn, handicap you as you struggle to make sense of what has happened.

The following steps are aimed at helping you to talk about an affair from the moment it is revealed:

STEP 1

Ideally, you should always tell your partner yourself if you have had an affair. Although people do discover affairs in lots of other ways (see pages 161–66) it is much better if the person who has had the affair explains what has happened. Making the decision to do this is not easy, but many people I have seen in counselling say that they knew the time was right. This may be because living a dual life – feeling guilty or fearing being discovered – was too hard to handle. Sometimes you may wish to tell because you feel it will definitely end the relationship, and this is what you desire. At other times the revelation of an affair can 'jump-start' a relationship because it causes you both to reassess your commitment, although a lot of soul searching is likely to go on before you reach this point. If repeated affairs are a facet of your relationship, you should still try to explain why another affair has taken place rather than assume that your partner has heard it all before.

Here are some guidelines for how to first tell and hear about an affair:

The Person Who Has Had the Affair

➤ Choose a venue where you are unlikely to be disturbed.

➤ Make time available rather than rush through your discussion because you have to leave.

➤ Be honest. Explain that you have something difficult to say and then say, 'I have had an affair.' Avoid using euphemisms such as 'I have someone else' or 'I feel strongly for another person', as they may be confusing for your partner.

➤ Avoid the intimate details of the affair at this stage. For instance, do not go into detail about the wonderful sex or weekend in a hotel. Your partner will be having a hard enough time getting to grips with the idea that you have had an affair, let alone the nitty-gritty of the relationship.

➤ Offer an explanation of why you think the affair happened. Avoid putting all the blame on your partner. For instance, do not say, 'If you had only been more attentive I would not have needed to confide in him/her.' Instead, explain any of the contributory issues that are appropriate and truthful. For example, you might say, 'I have been under terrific pressure at work that we did not talk about much. She/he was supportive and an affair developed.'

The Person Who Has Not Had the Affair

➤ Sit or stand so that you can maintain eye contact with your partner.

➤ Agree to spend appropriate time talking and listening to your partner, even if you fear bad news is at hand.

➤ Avoid cutting in on what your partner is saying. Let them finish before responding. You will probably be upset, but try not to start shouting or rush out. You need to hear the full story in order to assess exactly what has happened.

➤ Ask questions if you need to, but ask those that relate to why the affair happened. For instance, ask what your partner felt was going on in your relationship to warrant an affair. Avoid asking questions such as, 'Was she better in bed than me?' You may want answers to these later on, but it is better to try to make sense of your feelings about why the affair happened at this stage.

➤ Avoid immediately blaming your partner, their lover or yourself. It may seem tempting to hurl an insult at your partner about their fickleness and blame their lover as a seducer and man/woman hunter, but this will not help you to work out why the affair has happened. You should also shy away from self-blame. You may wonder if your own shortcomings have caused the affair, but ultimately affairs are at least the responsibility of your joint relationship and should not be regarded as just your (or your partner's) fault.

STEP 2

Now that you have told and heard the details of the affair, you will experience a whole range of emotions. The first feeling is usually shock. You may feel distanced from your surroundings, or as if the whole thing is happening to someone else. This is not only true for the person hearing about the affair. If you are reporting the affair, your nerves may cause you to experience some of the problems associated with shock. You could stumble over your words, or be unable to respond to your partner's questions. This is understandable, so it is important to build in some quiet time to allow the initial shock to pass. It is important to remain as calm as possible. This may seem tough in the face of the hurt and anger that normally follow shock, but allowing yourself to remain calm will enable you to deal more effectively with the situation.

STEP 3

A whole raft of emotions may also assail you both once the shock of hearing or telling the news has passed. Some people respond by feeling aggressive and extremely angry (although it is very unwise to carry out a desire to be violent). Others may break down in tears or feel shut off from their feelings. Whatever you feel is real and appropriate to you at that moment.

If you found out about the affair by reading a letter or overhearing a telephone conversation between your partner and their lover, for example, you may have dreaded, and yet wanted, confirmation of the affair. You may arrive at the discussion about the affair in a highly overwrought state, perhaps because you have had to initiate the discussion. Your overwhelming wish may simply be to hear the truth, and this can cause you to experience extremes of emotion before you hear anything from your partner. You may both be taken by surprise at the gale-force effect of the feelings you experience, and wonder how you can survive the next hour, let alone the rest of your relationship together.

You may not want your partner to touch you or offer any comfort (although some couples I have counselled have actually comforted each other because they felt sorry for the hurt that had been caused). Actions taken at this point can be extreme, as in the famous case of the woman who cut up all her husband's suits and gave away the contents of his wine cellar. Such actions are not recommended for the simple reason that they are nearly always regretted. If the relationship has any chance of continuing, this kind of behaviour will normally make it much more difficult to get it back on track. If it ends, acts of vengeance can leave a legacy of guilt and shame. They can also break down a sense of self-esteem. I have counselled people who took such action after the discovery of an affair, only to feel that they had let themselves down. If you need some kind of vindication the best advice is to live well and remain a person who can survive the onslaught of an affair with dignity.

STEP 4

This usually follows after a few days, although it can vary according to the individual couple. The time lapse allows for more focused thoughts and feelings to emerge. It is at this point that couples tend to begin to talk about the actual events of the affair, often accompanied by arguing and ultimatums. For instance, the partner who has not had the affair may demand that their partner does not sleep with them or moves out of the family home. Some people make snap decisions about the future of the relationship, deciding to stay together come what may or, more often, deciding that the affair has so destabilised the relationship that they must part.

It is natural to want to take positive action when everything about the two of you seems in turmoil. Doing something – anything – can appear to help dampen down the agony of indecision, confusion and uncertainty that follows an affair, but it is a false comforter. It is better to live with ambiguity about the future of the relationship for a while than seize upon a quick answer. This is for a number of reasons. Firstly, if you have children, splitting up and then changing your mind is very hard for them to handle. Secondly, you have not had enough time to decide what is the right thing to do. You may break up, but you may decide you can weather the affair if you work at the relationship. Your decisions may depend on the type of affair. For example, Josie forgave her boyfriend Eddie after a one-night stand at the start of their relationship, but could not tolerate his longer-term affair after they had been together five years and had a baby. You need time to think all this through, although it may be reasonable to take some decisions, such as deciding to sleep apart, until you have talked about the implications of the affair.

STEP 5

As a week or so passes, and if you are the partner who did not have the affair, you may become increasingly curious. You may find yourself asking questions about the affair, even though you know it will hurt to hear the answers. (This is similar to probing a wound to see if it still hurts.) This happens because you are gradually taking stock of what has happened

– carrying out a 'collateral damage check' and attempting to assess how deeply you and the relationship have been hurt by the affair.

You may experience the twin feelings of wanting to know, but also not wanting to know, exactly what happened. You will probably ask questions about the lover, wanting to know details of their behaviour and character. In some circumstances, you may do this because you want to let your partner off the hook and are seeking someone to blame for the affair. In other situations, you may be comparing yourself unfavourably with the lover, deciding that the affair was really your fault because you were not handsome enough or were too preoccupied with the family.

It is also at this point that you may begin to tell friends about the affair. Most people who do this do so because they want support and compassion. Given that they can no longer look to their partner for this, they turn to friends. This can be dangerous, particularly if your friends side with you against the person who has had the affair. If this happens you can feel justified in blaming your partner without thinking about how your actions might have contributed to the affair occurring. For instance, Frank told his best friend Derek about his wife, Gina, and her affair with a man she had met at her sports club. Frank was upset and angry, and Derek agreed with him that Gina had behaved abominably. Frank, however, did not tell Derek that he had had several affairs in the past.

In this situation Frank sought justification for feeling angry with Gina and used Derek to achieve it. He may have done this to avoid his own feelings of guilt over his affairs. You should also remember that you will permanently colour your friend's opinion of your partner, even though the two of you may eventually decide to stay together. At all costs, avoid spreading the news on the Internet, especially if you have children who could read the news on the website. This is also true of sharing news of the affair with other members of the family or workmates. You will have to manage the tricky balance of choosing very carefully whom you talk to and when to remain silent. As a rule of thumb, only choose people you really trust and who will give you support rather than take sides against either one of you.

STEP 6

In the first two weeks after the affair is revealed, you may find yourself wondering about the future of the relationship. Most people assume that an affair automatically ends a partnership. In fact, lots of people survive them. Your closest friends may have survived affairs that you know nothing about. (In Chapter 9 there is specific information about how to decide if the relationship can continue after an affair.) The best general advice at this stage is to suggest that you both take your time over this crucial issue. As Step 4 indicates, speedy decisions can cause more trouble than they are worth. This, of course, does not mean that you should not express your strong feelings (without violence or aggression) about the affair. You would not be human if you did not want your partner to know exactly how you feel about the effect of the affair on you, and on the family if you have one.

You might experience a mixture of these emotions in the immediate aftermath of finding out about an affair. They may follow each other in the order that the above steps describe, or appear to be mixed together in a random manner. This is natural because of the shock and disturbance to your partnership.

In the next chapter you can learn more about the way in which all three people in the 'affair triangle' may react to the affair being discovered, and how best to manage some of these feelings and behaviours.

CHAPTER 8

Now You Know: The Long-term Impact of an Affair

Once the shock of discovery has registered, you are likely to go through a number of feelings in the months that follow. Some are more pertinent if you are trying to stay together, but most can apply to those who experience affairs regardless of whether they stay in their committed relationship or not.

FEELINGS YOU MAY EXPERIENCE

IF YOU ARE THE PARTNER OF SOMEONE WHO HAD AN AFFAIR

Anger
You may feel so angry that it eats away at you. Sometimes the anger is not eased by shouting or accusing, but feels like a physical pain that never goes away. If you are trying to restore the relationship, this anger may build up inside you, preventing you from explaining how you feel. You could also fear that if you vent your anger it will become uncontrollable and so repress the feelings you experience.

Grief
Of all the feelings that you may experience after an affair, this is perhaps the longest lived and hardest to recover from. In a very real sense you are recovering from a death – the death of

your relationship. Even if the relationship improves and you stay together, it will never be the same again. You will experience all the feelings that you would expect to feel when someone dies – sadness, disbelief, a yearning to return to what has been lost, and depression.

Uncertainty

For a long time after an affair you may feel as if even simple decisions are hard to make. Many people, sometimes several months after an affair, describe a feeling of confusion and fear about doing or saying the wrong thing. You may feel as if all the criteria you previously made decisions on are no longer valid, but equally you do not know what is a solid base to build on.

Relief

If you have had suspicions about the affair, you may feel relieved that it is finally out in the open, rather than a secret that you have been afraid to broach.

Anxiety

After an affair is revealed you may experience the physical feelings associated with anxiety as well as the mental effects of worry. You could feel unwell and shaky, with an upset stomach, headaches and disturbances to your eating and sleeping patterns. You may also find the fact of the affair going round in your head, but never reaching a conclusion about what you want to do now.

Mistrust

Most people experience this as a long-term effect after an affair. You may find yourself struggling to believe what your partner tells you, perhaps feeling tempted to follow them when they go out, or demand confirmation of their plans.

Jealousy

You may find yourself feeling very jealous of the lover and the experiences your partner had with them. Sometimes the feelings focus on sex and what the sex was like, or about the actual person your partner had the affair with.

IF YOU ARE THE PERSON WHO HAD THE AFFAIR

Embarrassment

Facing up to explaining what you have done can be extremely embarrassing. You may have to own up to secrets and lies over a long period, and this can be very hard to do.

Loss

It may be difficult to acknowledge openly, but when you give up the affair you will probably miss the person, particularly if it was a long-standing relationship. This can feel like a deep loss. Sometimes you may miss what the person represented to you – escape from the everyday, sexual passion or just someone to talk to. You may also experience a feeling of loss about your committed relationship, wondering if it will ever be the same again.

Defensiveness

If your partner is jealous of your lover, you may find yourself spending a lot of time defending her or him. You could also worry that your partner will seek them out to attack, verbally or physically.

Avoidance

You may find yourself making excuses for the affair, or feel a longing to stop having to talk about it. You may decide that saying sorry is enough, and that your partner should be satisfied with your admission of the affair. You could find that if any discussion gets close to the topic of the affair you shy away from talking about it – perhaps leaving the room or changing the subject.

Stress and Anxiety

The person who has had the affair may also experience the effects of anxiety, including all the physical and mental problems described above. You may also wonder how long the feelings are going to last and long to get back to normal.

Self-reproach

If the affair was out of character for you, or perhaps you realised it was a mistake very quickly, you can blame yourself for acting in a way you now regret. You may not be able to shake off the feeling of guilt and sadness about the affair.

Confusion

Feeling confused about the future is common for the person who has had the affair. You may feel as if your whole life has been turned upside down, or feel very little and find it hard to empathise with your partner. Even if you decide to end the affair, you may wonder if you have done the right thing.

MANAGING FEELINGS AFTER AN AFFAIR

As you can see from the above, both partners have a lot of different emotions to deal with after an affair. At times, one partner may echo the other, with both feeling similar emotions. At other times partners may cross each other, with one partner feeling one thing while the other feels another. This can lead to communication blocks and arguments because they cannot empathise with each other.

> Stella and Ben are trying to recover from Ben's affair. A successful businessman with a workaholic lifestyle, Ben had fallen for the cliché of carrying on a six-month affair with his PA. The affair has recently come to light through Stella being told by a friend who had noticed the relationship at a

social event Ben was attending. Stella is desperately hurt and wants assurances from Ben that the affair is over for good. Ben is confused. He misses Debbie, his PA, whom he has agreed not to see, and is unsure whether he has done the right thing. Ben and Stella have found the weeks and months since the affair extremely difficult. They find it hard to have a normal conversation, let alone discuss the affair. Finally they reach a stalemate, where neither of them really makes contact with the other and they feel trapped in a world of their own.

Like Ben and Stella, it is all too easy to find tackling the affair difficult and so fall back to an emotional 'no man's land' where nothing in the relationship can either move forward or return to how it was. In fact, many couples who come to Relate for counselling ask for their relationship to be 'the same way it was before'. This is not possible. The revelation of the affair will have changed everything about the relationship, so that the partnership that once existed will have ceased to exist in every way that really matters.

KEY TASKS

Mourn For What Has Been Lost

Whether the couple ultimately stays together or splits up is irrelevant to the importance of this mourning period. Each member of the couple, alone and together, needs to grieve for the loss of the relationship. Not only do they need to mourn for what has been lost, but they must also let go of the expectations they had for the relationship in the future. This is why they may go through some of the same feelings experienced when a loved one dies. Sadness, anger and a longing for the more secure past are all associated with grieving and are natural responses to a difficult situation.

Assess the Damage to the Relationship

Affairs have different effects on different people. Some individuals react by immediately wanting the relationship to end (although speedy decisions are not generally useful). Some people may feel they can tolerate the affair, whilst others feel that the affair, once the dust has settled, has taught them a valuable lesson about changes they should make to improve the partnership. Attempting to assess what the affair means to each person and the partnership can help to quell the feelings of uncertainty and confusion that follow an affair.

Understand Why the Affair Happened

Of all the issues facing a couple after an affair this is the most important. If the reasons for the affair can be understood, and grappled with, then the affair will not have been completely senseless. Even if the affair proves to be a 'door opener' or an 'experimental' affair, at least both members of the couple will have understood what happened and why. This is not only crucial to the current relationship but also to any future relationships if the present one ends. Important relationship lessons can be learnt through understanding the affair. Knowing why an affair occurred can help a new relationship to be an improvement on the one that ended through an affair.

COPING WITH THE GRIEVING PROCESS

Accept that you need to mourn the relationship that has been changed forever by the affair. Some couples may avoid dealing with this because they want to present a face to the world that says, 'Nothing is wrong.' If the relationship has ended, you may not want to face the reality of the sadness you feel because you are angry about what has happened and want to tell friends you are glad the relationship is over and that you have got rid of the partner who hurt you. Most people find ambiguity hard to cope with. We like to be able to say 'It's over' or

'We're okay now' rather than 'Some days it's okay and other days I feel terrible'. Honestly admitting to feelings of loss can be a first step towards dealing with the uncertainty that often surrounds an affair.

The following ideas will help you to accept the grief you are likely to feel:

Keep a Journal

Writing down your feelings from day to day can help you to express them when you may find it hard to share them with anyone else. Looking back over the journal can help you to see patterns in your emotions, and that you have good days as well as bad. Research has found that keeping a journal can have beneficial effects for people suffering from illnesses such as depression, asthma and arthritis, so it could also help if you develop some of the physical symptoms of stress. If you do not like writing, try taping a journal as an alternative. Keep your journal in a safe place and update it when you need to. If you keep it on your computer, protect the file with a password. Remember, it is for your eyes only.

Talk to Someone You Trust About Your Feelings

Telling others how you feel can really help you to let go of the emotions. People who grieve often want to tell their story over and over again. This is an important part of mourning and can act as a release for pent-up emotions. *Always* choose a friend you can trust absolutely and who is unlikely to take sides against your partner. Someone who is willing to listen patiently is ideal, rather than a friend who interrupts with their own ideas about what has happened. Counselling can also be extremely helpful because the counsellor will allow you to say whatever is important to you without being judgmental or offering their personal point of view.

Be Kind to Yourself

Do not tell yourself that you must rush back to work or behave as if nothing has happened. Something important *has* happened and you need time to process it. It can help to talk to your HR department, who may be able to arrange leave for you. Your GP could also be a useful contact as you may need sick leave to deal with the emotions you are feeling.

Relax more, but keep a routine going. Something simple, like cooking a meal or always walking to the newsagent to get the paper at the same time every day, can help you to manage the day more effectively. If you want to cry, allow yourself to do this. Some people find watching a weepy film helpful because it allows the tears to fall rather than being bottled up. Vent angry feelings by beating pillows piled on the bed with a rolled-up newspaper or taking lots of glass to the bottle bank to recycle. Smash the glass with vigour as you post it through the slot in the bank! Other ways of allowing angry feelings to come out safely are to walk rather than drive everywhere, join a gym or take up any sport that allows you to be physically active. Increasing physical activity is a proven way of dispersing stress and aggression. If you have mobility problems, do any physical activity that is slightly stretching and different to your usual routine.

Allow Yourself to Feel Sad if You Have Ended a Relationship with a Lover

If you have decided to end the relationship with a lover you may feel guilty about being sad about the loss. You may have made this decision for the best of reasons – to try to rebuild your partnership, care for children or because you are unsure about how you feel – but this does not mean you will not miss the company of the person you had the affair with. Explaining these feelings to your partner can be very difficult, but you could seek counselling to help you manage the loss, particularly if your partner finds this issue hard to understand.

Share the Feelings of Loss with Your Partner

If you are trying to cope with the aftermath of an affair you may want to soldier on alone. This can happen partly because trusting your partner after such a breach of trust has made you wary, and partly because sharing your feelings may seem to make you vulnerable to being hurt again. If, however, you attempt to share something of what you are feeling it can help your partner to understand the impact of the affair, and will improve the chances of you communicating successfully about why the affair happened in the first place.

DANGER SIGNS OF DEPRESSION

Strong feelings of unhappiness are usual after an affair. It is necessary to seek expert medical help if any of the following occur because they could be symptoms of depression, as opposed to 'feeling low' or miserable.

Long-term Changes in Sleeping and Eating Habits

Depressed people often wake very early in the morning with a sense of dread or find getting to sleep very difficult. Alternatively, the desire to sleep all the time can be a symptom of depression. Eating very little or overeating for a period of time longer than a few weeks can also indicate depression, particularly if this is a change to normal behaviour. See your GP if this describes you or your partner.

An Inability to Connect with Daily Life

If the person seems withdrawn and silent, and this is a change from their normal behaviour, help should be sought if the withdrawal lasts for several weeks. Problems with washing, dressing or carrying out a simple daily routine can also indicate depression and should be investigated by a medical professional.

Mood Swings

Most people experience changes in mood, but if these are excessive – crying one moment and shouting the next – and carry on for more than a couple of months, seek assistance from your GP or other health professional.

Talking About Committing Suicide

There is an urban myth that if a person talks about suicide they will not actually carry the intention through. This is not true. If a person has got as far as talking about suicide, and also discusses how they intend to carry it out, it is vital to contact a medical professional. You could also gain advice and support from the Samaritans (telephone 0345 909090 or e-mail jo@samaritans.org.uk).

HOW TO ASSESS THE DAMAGE
TO YOUR RELATIONSHIP

If you are to make any kind of decision about the future for the two of you, you will need to assess exactly what the affair means to you. This is not an easy task because it will require you to communicate successfully when you both probably want to avoid talking to each other about the affair. If, however, you are going to move forward rather than remain stuck, you must attempt this. You also need to avoid arguing and bickering as much as possible. Fighting usually ends up with both of you stuck behind high emotionally defensive walls that will prevent you from resolving anything.

Use the following steps to make a personal and relationship damage assessment.

MAKE A LIST

Make a list of what would need to change if the relationship is to carry on. Some changes may be small – such as always coming home from work on time. Others will be larger – such as always keeping promises or agreeing never to see the lover again. Be specific rather than general. For example, do not say, 'I would like more affection.' Instead say, 'I would like to have a kiss when I come home from work or for us to cuddle each other in bed.'

Once you have completed your lists, share them with each other. Ask your partner if they think they can agree to most of the list or only a little. Agreeing to only a small number of items may not indicate the relationship is over, but it could suggest that a lot of hard work lies ahead if the relationship is to succeed. Once you have drawn up the list of possible changes, talk about what would help them to become reality. Again, be specific about any changes you wish to make. Say, 'I would like us to spend at least two evenings a week together without watching television or socialising with other people,' rather than, 'We should have more time together.' In this way, if you can be focused about what you decide to do, you will know when you have not achieved your goals. Giving vague promises or agreeing to a grand scheme that lacks real substance leaves lots of room for arguing and disagreeing about what you actually signed up to. Check out every couple of weeks whether you agree you have met your goals and make changes if this does not seem to be happening.

This approach can also work if you realise that the relationship is going to end. Use your list to decide what will need to happen if you are to part with as little acrimony as possible. This is particularly important if you have children. They need your loving concern rather than being the helpless witnesses to a parental battle as you split up.

THINK ABOUT YOURSELF

Your relationship is not the only thing that has taken a battering. At a personal level you are likely to be suffering a loss of self-esteem. This usually occurs because admitting to, or hearing about, an affair causes you to doubt what you thought you knew about yourself and your ability to make accurate judgments about other people. Some couples tell Relate counsellors that it can feel like the carpet has been pulled out from under their feet; as if everything they based their decision-making on has been false. You may also find yourself wondering if you can be the person you thought you were – especially if you have had a one-night stand and now regret this or have realised that you did not recognise the signs of the long-term affair in your partner. Now is the time to consider what would help to restore your self-esteem. Think about the things that usually help you to feel good about yourself – physically and mentally – and build these into your life.

For instance, Sheila felt knocked for six when her husband of 20 years left her for another woman. After the immediate impact had abated somewhat, Sheila volunteered to help at a local hospice. She found this immensely rewarding with the additional bonus that, because she felt of value to the hospice, her self-esteem improved dramatically.

If your sexual self-image has been crushed because a partner has had sex with someone else you may be tempted to rush into a new relationship to reassure yourself that you are sexy and attractive. This is not advisable. Taking this kind of action is rather like sticking a plaster over a gaping wound. It is better to wait until you have understood more about why the affair happened and recovered from the shock. You will then be better equipped to manage a new relationship, especially a sexual one.

UNDERSTANDING WHY THE AFFAIR HAPPENED

After an affair it may seem clear what the problem is: you or your partner has been unfaithful. If you just settle for this obvious explanation, though, you will miss a real opportunity to understand what caused the affair. Affairs are symptoms, not causes. Why is it important to understand what happened? Because you can only repair the damage once you know what has underpinned the affair. Imagine repairing the roof of a house when the walls are shaky and foundations crumbling. Pretty soon the roof would have no house to cover. It is like this with affairs. You may be able to patch things together for a while, but without overhauling the deeper reasons, the relationship may eventually collapse.

The following suggestions will help you to decide why the affair happened in your relationship:

WHAT WAS THE TRIGGER?

Sit down with your partner and discuss the events that occurred just before the affair began. Look for anything that seemed of note that happened in the relationship or family. As you read in Chapter 3, many affairs are prompted by change – bereavement, job loss or gain, pregnancy, parenting problems and so on. Look for these changes. You could also look further back in your relationship, as some issues connected to affairs can lie dormant in a partnership for a long time.

For instance, Bob and Deirdre had been married for eight years when Bob embarked on an affair with Deirdre's friend. When the affair came to light, Deirdre could not understand why it had happened. As far as she was concerned, the marriage was happy. When they began to talk about the affair, Bob explained that he had found that Deirdre's emotional withdrawal from him after she lost her job had left a scar. He had felt alienated. Although their relationship had improved after a year or so, he had never come to terms with his feeling that Deirdre did not fancy him any more. When Deirdre's friend had flirted with him, Bob enjoyed feeling desirable and began an affair with her.

You could also think about the issues you know have commonly been 'taboo' for you as a couple. For instance, do you know that the minute you start talking about his family a row ensues? Do you develop cold silences if you attempt to talk about money or sex? And what about any problems you have in talking to each other about your emotions and private thoughts? These kinds of concern can all contribute to a feeling that an affair is somehow justified. Self-justification is often one of the steps towards having an affair, but can also follow after an affair has started.

Unaddressed difficulties in a relationship may give a toehold to self-justification. For instance, Michael decided he would begin his affair when he told himself that his wife would barely notice because she was always working and hardly saw him. In fact, once the affair was discovered, his wife was very upset that Michael had not asked her to work less hard in order to spend more time with him.

USING THE KNOWLEDGE

Once you have discussed the important issues from the past that may have contributed to an affair, you can use the knowledge to alter your present relationship if you decide to go on together, or to remember for any future partnerships if you separate. This kind of learning can be painful, as you may want to defend yourself against accusations of not caring or seeming uninterested in the relationship in the past. It is worth sticking with, though, because ultimately the present, or any future, relationship will benefit greatly.

Talk about what you both expect from the relationship, and how this can be achieved. You might find it useful to utilise the 'list idea' from page 190. This time, add in the way you tackle change and difference and create this as a goal. For example, you might discover that the affair was caused, in part, by frequent arguments over who does what in the home. One partner may have become so irritated that they were expected to take on the lion's share of domestic tasks that they rebelled by sharing leisure time with someone else. A couple could use this knowledge to create the goal of being more equal in sharing the cleaning and cooking in the future so that neither partner becomes frustrated at being expected to clean up after the other. This could also be valuable learning if the couple parts and begins new relationships as they may decide to review early on with a new partner who has responsibility for housework.

There is another important reason to attempt to understand why the affair happened. The apportioning of blame is a common scenario when couples try to discuss an affair. One partner may blame the other for the affair or an individual may blame themselves for what happened. Neither of these is helpful. Relate counsellors can tell you that nearly all affairs are the result of difficulties in the way the couple has related to each other during the time they have been together. This means that the responsibility is shared, and needs to be tackled in a shared way, rather than pushed on to one or other of the couple.

MANAGING THE FALLOUT FROM AN AFFAIR

Ask the Questions You Can Bear to Hear the Answers To

When you first hear about an affair you may be tempted to ask a thousand questions. It is better to pace yourself when asking any questions, giving yourself time to approach the most difficult issues later on. If you are telling your partner about the affair, give the information in a way that your partner can understand, and answer questions in an honest and focused manner. For example, if your partner asks, 'Why have you done this?' answer by saying, 'Because I was lonely/confused/ jealous/felt shut out after the birth of our baby' (or whatever you feel gives some idea of why the affair occurred), rather than 'I don't know, it just happened', which explains nothing.

Agree Particular Times to Talk About the Affair

Talking about the affair can become all encompassing, particularly if you are exchanging insults or accusations. This often means that you both end up stressed and unable to talk in any meaningful way about what has happened. One way round this is to agree to talk about the affair for only half an hour a day. During this time, one person can ask questions or both can discuss the feelings they are experiencing. When the half-hour is up, the discussion should stop. This approach requires discipline, but helps to reduce the recriminations that inevitably fly around after an affair. At the end of any conversation, try to decide what you have gained from the discussion. It could even help to make a note of any issues you have discussed and made a decision about.

Don't Blame the Lover

Some couples cannot face the reality of the actions of the person who has had the affair and fix all the blame on the lover. Typically, they designate the lover as 'predatory', a 'seducer' or 'someone who sleeps around'. This may suit the person who has had the affair as it avoids them having to face up to their own culpability. It also means that the partner who did not have the affair can let their partner 'off the hook', thereby allowing all the responsibility for the affair to be carried by the lover. It is true that the lover has their own responsibilities in the situation, but if the relationship is to move forward in any direction, the couple must own up to the true reasons for the affair rather than hold another person completely responsible.

Be Prepared to Listen

Listening is a dying art. People tend to rush from one concern to another, often talking about their own issues rather than allowing space for others to respond. This can be true for couples, and especially so after an affair. Each partner may be so taken up with his or her personal view of the affair, and so keen to tell their partner about that view, that they forget to listen to what the other person is really saying. This can also happen if the partner who has had the affair feels guilty and so blocks attending to the effect of the affair on their partner. Listen carefully to your partner, maintaining eye contact and not interrupting until they have finished what they have to say. If they are upset, remain calm and offer reassurance rather than becoming upset yourself. Never accuse them of being stupid or making too much fuss. Their feelings are real for them, even if you do not agree with their viewpoint.

Give Yourself Time

Do not expect to resolve all the problems that an affair brings to the surface in a few weeks. Recovery from an affair can take months or years. Deal with each part of the process as it comes along and accept that feelings of grief, jealousy, anger and confusion are natural and appropriate, given the circumstances. You and your partner may long for the whole thing to be over, but this is unrealistic. Building trust can take a long time – years in some cases. Rebuilding broken trust can take longer, and it is this task you are attempting.

The first weeks and months after an affair is revealed can be the most agonising. If you use the suggestions in this chapter you may find that you can cope well enough to make the important decisions you now face, such as deciding whether the relationship can survive or how to talk to others about the affair. The next chapter deals with these issues, suggests helpful ways to talk to children and others about an affair, as well as taking a brief look at the role of the lover once the affair has been revealed.

CHAPTER 9

Recovery – Can We Make it?

When an affair has been revealed, the first weeks and months are painful and difficult. You may feel as if you are just existing from day to day; carrying out the usual routines but all the while feeling disorientated and unsure of what lies ahead. Some couples do break up almost immediately, while others hang on together for some time, trying to decide what to do. Even those who break up in the first days after an affair comes to light eventually need to make a long-term decision about the future. You are likely to ask yourself and your partner, 'Can we make it?'

Whether you stay together or part is the key question for this stage and depends somewhat on why the affair happened and the type of affair it was. For instance, a 'door opener' affair may mean that the chances of the relationship continuing are slim. An 'experimental' affair probably stands a reasonable chance of surviving, whereas a 'three-legged stool' affair may require a great deal of hard work by both partners if the relationship is to succeed. Of course, each affair is unique to the people who encounter it. What one couple can survive could break another. Only you will know how important the affair has been in your life.

TALKING ABOUT THE FUTURE OF THE RELATIONSHIP

Whatever the outcome, you both need to talk about the future of your relationship. It is crucial to make joint decisions about the future for some important reasons:

➤ If just one of you decides the relationship is over, and leaves, you will have acquired little or no understanding about why the affair happened. This may deny you valuable learning about making any future relationships more secure.

➤ If you have children, they deserve that you pay full attention to the future of the relationship. If you make a snap decision to stay or go based on the powerful emotions of the event you may reverse this later, with the consequence that your children will feel confused and destabilised.

➤ Discussing the future of your partnership can be a first step in building effective communication between you. This is an extremely useful skill to develop whether you stay together or part. If you need to go on being parents, even though you are unable to be partners, successful communication will smooth the way for your meetings in the future and help you to avoid arguments in front of the children.

HOW TO TALK ABOUT THE FUTURE

Choose a Good Time and Place

Fix a time when you will not be interrupted and you feel reasonably relaxed. Unplug the phone, turn off the television, mobile phone and laptop and avoid times when you know you are likely to be stressed or tired – such as late at night and immediately after work. You may find you need to sit at a table rather than on a sofa. You could also choose neutral ground, such as a quiet café, but you may feel constrained by the other people in hearing range. Make sure you can see each other easily and that you feel reasonably confident that your partner is listening and attending to you.

Decide How Long You Will Talk For

You may need a number of similar conversations to arrive at a final decision. It is better to have five one-hour conversations than one five-hour conversation. An hour is probably roughly the right amount of time. Longer than this can feel tiring, and if you go on for longer you will probably forget the details of your discussions.

Start By Discussing Your Options

Most couples who talk to Relate counsellors about affairs offer two options – staying or going. In fact, there are usually many options that come to light during counselling that the couple has not thought of. For each option, make a note on a piece of paper and lay it on the table or floor. Number them as you think of them. Try not to argue with your partner if you do not agree with their choice. Just make a note and add it to the others. For instance, here are some of the options that Carrie and Ivan came up with after Carrie's affair:

Option 1 – Carrie to leave and live with Keith, her lover, if Keith is willing.

Option 2 – Carrie to leave their shared home and live alone.

Option 3 – Ivan to leave their shared home and live alone.

Option 4 – Carrie and Ivan to go on living together and try to forget the affair.

Option 5 – Carrie and Ivan to go on living together with the proviso that they review the relationship in six months' time.

Option 6 – Carrie and Ivan to seek couple counselling to help them make sense of the affair.

Option 7 – Carrie and Ivan to accept the affair and Carrie to go on seeing Keith with Ivan's agreement.

Option 8 – Carrie and Ivan to move away from the area.

Option 9 – Carrie and Ivan to go on living together but alter the terms of their relationship so that they are free to have other relationships.

Option 10 – Carrie and Ivan to change from living together to being married.

The next step, once all the possible options have been explored and noted, is to begin weeding. Some of the options on the table are bound to strike you immediately as no good. For instance, Carrie and Ivan immediately rejected Options 9 and 7 as neither of them thought they could cope with these. Carrie explained to Ivan that Keith had told her that the relationship was over now that Ivan knew about it, so Option 1 was also rejected. Carrie felt that Option 4 was too difficult because the affair had had such a negative effect on them. Of the options left open to them they created a priority list, rating their favoured choices first and the least favoured last. Eventually they decided to list their options in the following way: Options 5, 6, 2, 3, 10 and 8.

This listing gave Carrie and Ivan interesting information about what they both expected from their future life. They were able to see that they wanted to try and rebuild the relationship and were willing to seek help to do this. They also identified the pain they were both feeling, as leaving remained an option after trying again. Marriage or moving was seen as too big a step, given the fragile nature of their relationship.

Listing options in this way can help you to feel less stuck and unsure about what you and your partner want, and can make some decisions very clear indeed. For instance, if Carrie and Ivan had both put Options 2 and 3 at the top of their list they would have realised that the future of the relationship was very unstable indeed.

Talk About What Action You Need to Take to Make Your Decisions Happen

If you have decided to divorce, for example, you may wish to see a solicitor. If you wish to stay together, talk about how you can recreate mutual trust. For instance, you may decide that you will always go to social events together from now on, turning down invitations for one partner alone. Carrie and Ivan agreed that Ivan would call Relate to make a counselling appointment, while Carrie promised to sever all links with Keith, and leave the accountancy class where they had first met.

Agree a Review Time

If you are to be sure that your hopes and expectations are really being fulfilled, you need to agree to review your decisions. Make a note of what you decided and keep it somewhere safe (you should both keep a copy of this). In deciding your review time, you need to strike a balance between constantly talking about whether things are going as you want or leaving it so long you have almost forgotten what you wanted to say to each other. Two to three months is probably a good gap to allow you time to begin the process of working on your relationship. You could do this even if you split up as you may wish to assess how you feel about the relationship now you are apart. It may also be extremely important for your future parenting responsibilities. At the review, talk about your decisions and decide if they still meet your needs. If necessary, add or remove any ideas that have obviously changed.

Sticking to this pattern until you feel more secure will help you to go on dealing with your feelings in a way that is practical and helpful, because it promotes control. From an emotional point of view, dealing with the long-term effect of an affair can feel like wrestling an octopus. Gaining a measure of control over the situation can buy you and your partner breathing space so that you both make the right decision at the right time. This is not to suggest that you become like Mr Spock in *Star Trek* in your responses – so sensible that all real emotion is ignored. You are bound to experience messy and raw feelings, but taking time to create a working structure will help you to improve your self-esteem as you will be able to feel proud that you have taken some steps to address the problems you face.

MANAGING JEALOUSY

As a Relate counsellor, I know that jealousy is often a big problem that couples encounter when they try to rebuild their partnership. Most jealousy comes from fear and a low sense of self-esteem. The fear that people experience is due to an anxiety that they will face repeating problems with their present (or future) partner. They may also fear that any fragile trust they build up will be destroyed again and that they will look foolish for sticking with a partner who is untrustworthy. Low self-esteem usually follows the revelation of an affair because the person who has been betrayed wonders if they really knew their partner, and consequently if they can go on believing in their own ability to make good judgments about other people. They may also feel less sexually attractive. This can lead to a situation where they retreat from a sexual relationship with the partner who has had the affair, but also want to demonstrate that they can be as good a sexual partner as the lover was. It is no wonder that jealousy is a complex subject that many couples find overwhelming and frightening.

Jamal and Asuka had found themselves recovering from a close friendship that Asuka had developed with a man at work. There had been no sexual relationship, but Jamal had been very upset to discover that Asuka had shared some intimate family secrets with her colleague. Jamal felt betrayed and he and Asuka went through a difficult time for some weeks as they talked about what had happened. Jamal began to question Asuka about what she did at work, and then to insist that he took her to and from work. Eventually he demanded that Asuka change her job, as he could not stand the thought of her seeing the man at her office. Asuka felt like a bird in a cage, and it was a long time before Asuka and Jamal began to have a relationship that was more open and trusting.

There are two main types of jealousy. The first kind is fairly natural. In this kind of jealousy you may be mildly concerned if your partner spends a lot of time at work or pays a lot of attention to another person. This feeling demonstrates that you want to be with your partner and care about them. Sometimes jealousy can be triggered by other members of the family, such as when your partner appears to care more about your child or their parent than you. Usually this kind of jealousy never amounts to much more than a minor irritation and passes off when you are able to spend more time together.

The second kind of jealousy is more serious and can affect you both so much that it is hard to carry on normal life. When this occurs, you may feel as if your whole life is dominated by the jealousy. If you are the person who has had the affair you may feel caged by your partner who constantly telephones to see where you are, refuses to let you out on your own and makes a scene if you have to go somewhere alone. If you are the person whose partner had an affair you may be gripped by the fear that they are about to find another partner at any time, despite their reassurances. You may spend time alone agonising about what they are doing; you may plan recriminations against the lover (and carry them out – such as scratching their car or writing malicious e-mails), or lay down impossible rules for your partner to adhere to. If this kind of jealousy carries on for a long time, it usually causes the partner who is the victim to want to leave, thereby forcing the very situation that the jealous person does not want. It is impossible to build a trusting relationship for the future if you are both unable to give or accept trust because of the jealousy.

FIGHTING JEALOUS FEELINGS

The best way to prevent destructive jealousy is to improve a sense of self-esteem. People who become obsessively jealous often do so because they have invested their whole self-image in their partner. Gradually you need to wean yourself away from the idea that life is only worth living if you have the partner you are currently with. You need to see your partner as a separate person who cannot be forced to love you but only gives love because they want to. Yes, you may worry that they are talking to a stranger at work or at the pub, but this is the nature of trust – you have to let go in order to hold on. Develop and nurture your own friendships and pursuits so that you have areas of life where you feel you are able and supported.

If you have been hurt by a partner's infidelity, the old proverb is still true – 'To live well is the best revenge'. Getting on with your life and making a success of things will help you to recover from an affair much more quickly than plotting how to avenge yourself on the lover – or making new demands of your partner.

If you are the person who had the affair, you will have to undertake to keep your promises, but you must only promise those things you know are achievable. For instance, Paula demanded that her husband Jeremy should return from work at exactly half-past six every evening so that she would know he was not meeting his girlfriend on the way home, as he had done for the previous four months. Jeremy told Paula he could not make such a promise. He explained that he might be asked to work late, be caught in a traffic jam or delayed on the train. Instead he promised to call her on his mobile phone to let her know exactly what was happening.

It goes without saying that if you promise to stop seeing a lover you must do this. Trust is not just in the promise, but also in the proof. If you intend to rebuild the relationship, you must carry out the actions you promise. You must also be truthful about the way you feel about the future of the relationship. If you are torn about seeing your lover or staying with your partner, do not voice platitudes about 'it all working out eventually' or tell lies about your intentions. It is better to say honestly that you are uncertain, because jealousy often feeds on the hidden feelings between you that are difficult to voice.

REBUILDING YOUR SEX LIFE

If you decide to stay together you may find that sex is the area that causes you the biggest problems. After time, you might feel confident about day-to-day matters, such as managing child-care and money, and communication between you may have improved. However, many couples still encounter problems with sex many months after the affair came out. This is usually because of the intimacy of lovemaking.

If you care about someone in a relationship, and have made love over a long period of time with them, you will have let your emotional guard down. Your union is more than just the bodily act of having sex – a physically enjoyable activity, but some-times not as satisfying as the emotional closeness that takes years to develop. An affair knocks a huge hole in this closeness, so restoring it can take a long time. As explained earlier, some people in affairs notice a resurgence of sexual desire because the intimacy with a lover stimulates their interest in sex. Whatever happens, though, most couples struggle with sex after an affair because of anger, jealousy, feelings of inadequacy, guilt and anxiety. Here are some things you can do to lessen this experience, and strengthen your loving bond to one another.

START SLOWLY

Work on your everyday affection. Share a kiss or hug, be encouraging to each other and spend plenty of time together as a couple. It might help to give up thinking about lovemaking for some time, even if you know you want to stay together. Instead, try to boost the sense of warmth in the partnership so you feel close to one another.

DO SPECIAL THINGS TOGETHER

Find things that you would both enjoy, especially things you know your partner would never have done with their lover. For instance, find a different restaurant you both like, watch a new film or DVD that was not out when the affair occurred, and take the children on a trip as a family. These may not seem immediately connected to sex, but the sense of closeness lays the foundations for successful sex in the relationship.

BE HONEST ABOUT HOW YOU ARE FEELING

Some couples feel they have to put on a sexual pretence, especially if everything else in the relationship is gradually recovering. They may fear that if they say 'I am having trouble enjoying sex because I find I am thinking about the other man/woman' that their partner will start looking for someone else. If this affects you, just say you need to take things slowly. Be considerate of each other, rather than trying to conform to ideas about sex that are not working for you any more.

EXPERIMENT WITH NEW THINGS

Think about doing more touching and caressing, kissing and lying quietly together. If your trust has been hurt you need sex that is affirming and loving rather than some new wild sexual technique. Try longer sessions of stroking and massaging the whole body, brushing each other's hair and feeding one another with favourite foods – strawberries, chocolate and ice cream can be erotic and fun.

Try Text Sex

Using text to flirt or arouse can be a powerful way of connecting with your partner. It has a directness that can speak to the heart, and the possibility of being re-read and delighted in for as long as you choose to keep the text or e-mail. It can be a real way of maintaining intimacy if you are apart for some time – perhaps if one of you is on a business trip, for instance. It's true that nothing beats face-to-face contact, but texting and e-mailing can meet your needs when personal contact is not possible. You can also use it to boost a dull day or just to let your partner know you are thinking of them. Use the following guidelines to help you navigate some of the drawbacks you might encounter.

Keep the Messages Private

It's surprising how many people discover that their partner has shown a friend a sexy text or picture that was never meant for public display. Be aware that your children or visitors to your home could read the texts if you leave the phone unattended. If necessary, protect your phone with a PIN or password.

Use Acceptable Words and Images

Agree what turns you on and what would cause you offence. Keep your texts at the same acceptability level. Don't try and push a partner to be raunchier if they are not ready for it, or demand they try out new things just to please you.

Get the Timing Right

Never send messages at a time you know could be compromising for your partner. Receiving a sexy message in their lunch hour at work might be okay, but not if you think they could be in a busy meeting! If you want text sex to lead to lovemaking when you meet this should be negotiated. Expecting your partner to be red hot for action when they have spent the day with a crying baby or had back-to-back meetings at work is asking for trouble. Pick your moment to exchange sexy texts. You could even begin by asking how their day is and how they are feeling to test the water before sending anything more sexually provocative. You could also offer to give a massage or run them a soothing bath before lovemaking to alleviate any stress their day has held.

Be Cautious with Images

You might find using pictures from websites or social net-working sites arousing, but your partner may not. Stick to personal messages. If you are going to use photos of your body, think about how well you know each other and where this picture could end up. You definitely do not want to find yourself half-naked on YouTube. Only send intimate pictures if you absolutely trust each other, and then only if you know your partner will enjoy them. I have heard of a woman meeting a new man for a date for the first time, only to receive a naked picture from him the next day. Needless to say, she was not impressed. Not only did the picture reveal a less than sexy body, but she also felt it was way too much too soon. Also, the idea of the naked photo shoot can often follow drinking too much – beware the boozy topless shot. In the morning, this will not look so good, especially if your beloved has shared it with all their friends on a social networking site.

Start by Being Romantic

Using romantic and seductive language at first is better than going straight into sexed-up mode. As with face-to-face encounters, racing straight into wild sex can feel uncomfortable if you are not used to it. Remember, the idea is to build a sense of being wanted and loved rather than sex for its own sake. Showing you care and want to connect to your partner is as important as exciting them sexually at a distance. Also, if you want the messaging to be a lead-up to actual lovemaking when you meet, putting them off at this stage will end all your hopes.

Use Explicit Language Carefully

Rather than use it every other word, try using explicit language as a surprise when texting a longer message about how you feel about your partner. This shock factor can arouse more effectively than a semi-pornographic message, which can make many people switch off. If you have pet names for parts of your partner's body, mix these with earthier terms to encourage a feeling of individuality and specialness.

Text Little and Often

Texting little and often is the best way to let your partner know you are thinking of them in a flirty way. Long texts with loads of lists containing '. . . and the next thing I'm going to do is . . .' are not arousing, just boring. Instead, a text that says 'I would love to be kissing your breast/bottom now' is more flirtily naughty and gets straight to the point.

Use the Delete Button

You may find the texts and/or pictures exciting, but to avoid inadvertently sending a raunchy picture to your mother-in-law (yes, it has happened) get rid of the texts you really do not need to keep.

FIND TIMES TO BE INTIMATE

Put time aside for lovemaking rather than hope it will happen of its own accord. Decide to have an evening in, minimise distractions and make sure the kids are asleep. Shut the door and just enjoy the freedom to be close to one another. If it takes some time to feel confident about sex, do not rush things. If you are the partner who had the affair you may find that feelings of guilt or embarrassment cause you to feel uncomfortable. If you did not have the affair, you may feel angry or upset about your partner having sex with someone else. All this takes time to resolve. Keep working on being close to one another.

BE FORGIVING OF YOURSELF

If you find sex difficult, do not push yourself into making love because you think you ought to – perhaps to prove to your partner that you love them or that you are over the affair, for instance. If you do not make love when you expected to, or it does not prove satisfying, just look forward to the next time. Not all lovemaking can be earth-moving. In fact, being intimate needs variety, so sometimes a gentle low-key experience is good, while at other times you will want passion and thrill. Go with the flow of your mood and try to read each other's feelings.

BE WARY OF REBOUND SEX

When you first decide to stay together, or even if you are uncertain whether you want to, you may find you want to have sex a lot. This desire can feel overwhelming, as if you feel compelled to make love. Sometimes this is due to the strong emotions that have probably been flying around as the affair is revealed. Anger and sadness, surprisingly, are often expressed in lovemaking. You may also use sex to express your relief that your partner has not immediately left the family. Be careful, though, because if you rush into several weeks of heated sex, only to eventually separate, you may regret this style of expression. Before embarking on this kind of sex, ask yourself what you want from the sex and why you are doing it. You do not have to be self-critical, only self-analytical. Have an eye on the future as you take the decision to go to bed with a partner who has just revealed an affair, or to whom you have just admitted an affair.

TALKING TO OTHERS ABOUT THE AFFAIR

TELLING YOUR CHILDREN

Telling your children that one of you has had an affair may be one of the most difficult tasks you ever have to undertake. Whether your child is small, a teenager or even an adult, you will be admitting to something that most children find hard to accept about a parent. This is because children want to see their parents as caring people who would not willingly deceive another. In children of around six or seven this can be most acute because children of this age group tend to develop hero worship of their parents.

Despite the difficulties, you may have to say something to your children, particularly if the affair becomes common knowledge. It is much better that they hear it from you than from a friend in the playground who has heard it from their parents. It is crucial that you have a really good reason for telling them – perhaps if one partner is leaving. Never use your child as a sounding board for your own unhappy feelings. They are not mature enough to manage this load. If you need to talk, find a counsellor.

Use the following guidelines to help you tell your children:

Tell Them All Together and as a Couple

If you tell just one child at a time, or leave breaking the news to one partner alone, you can set up problems. They may feel they should take one partner's side against the other, or keep the affair a secret from the other children, which is too heavy a burden for most children.

Keep the Information Simple

Tell your children in terms that they can easily understand. Explain that you have had a close friendship with someone else and that this has caused you and your partner to feel unhappy. If you have not made up your mind about staying or going, do not make a promise about staying if you are not sure what will happen. As with a partner, only promise what you can deliver.

Reassure the Children That You Love Them

Children need to know that, even in the worst situations, they are still loved and cared for. Explain that although you do not know what is going to happen, you still love them and want the best for them.

Answer Their Questions Honestly

Your children will want to ask you questions about what has happened. Be truthful, but do not go into great detail about meeting the new partner. Instead, give any details that are pertinent to them rather than you.

Do Not Rubbish Your Partner

You may be tempted to denigrate your partner, but this is a bad idea. Your child needs to go on having a relationship with both of you, whatever you feel. You should never use your children as go-betweens for the two of you if you are not talking. Your child is not a messenger and should not be asked to carry the emotional burden of delivering messages between the two of you.

TALKING TO FAMILY AND FRIENDS

Many of the guidelines for talking to children about an affair also apply when talking to adults. Be straightforward and honest, giving the information as you know it. To avoid setting up recrimination, tell your friends and family the same thing at the same time. If you do not do this you may find that they take sides against you, your partner or each other. It is likely that you will not be able to avoid some relations and friends being polarised, but if you can minimise this it will help after the affair.

It is common for Relate counsellors to see individuals who have had an affair with one of their relatives, especially in-laws. For instance, they may have had an affair with their partner's brother or sister. This also happens with close friends. On the face of it, this can seem the worst betrayal of all. The two people you trust most have let you down in a dramatic way. The person who has not had the affair may say, 'How can they have done this?' but it is not so strange. The chances are that you have chosen your friends because they share the same interests as you, and that your relatives have much in common with you. Your partner may have been attracted by precisely these shared elements.

Unfortunately, this kind of alliance can split a family apart, sometimes resulting in an estrangement between parent and adult child. The couple may also have to live with seeing the person with whom the affair happened at family gatherings. This can be very hard to bear so the couple may eventually cut themselves off from the family. As with all affairs, it is important to recognise the deep-seated reasons for the affair in this situation. Understanding what has happened, and why, can help you all to cope. It is better, however, to resist the temptation to have an affair with a close friend or family member because of the ripples of pain it can spread throughout many people's lives. No affair is to be recommended as a course of action, but this kind can be devastating to deal with in the long run.

THE ROLE OF THE LOVER

This book has chiefly been aimed at the couple who embark on, and then have to deal with, an affair, but it is worth briefly mentioning the lover and the role they may take in the affair.

There are lots of myths around people who have a relationship with someone who is already in a committed relationship. If it is a man, he may be seen as a 'jack-the-lad' who has little feeling about starting a relationship with a woman already in a partnership. If it is a woman she may be regarded as a 'tart' or a 'sexual siren' to whom men are attracted against their better instincts. None of these images are true. Usually they are people who meet an individual they are attracted to in the same way as anybody else. They may feel that the person they have the affair with must make up their own mind about being faithful, or simply block the knowledge of the committed relationship because they want the relationship so much.

THE COMMITMENT-PHOBIC LOVER

There is, however, a common thread that perhaps describes the kind of person who knows that their chosen lover is already in a committed relationship but goes ahead nevertheless. They may be 'commitment phobic' – that is they are actually attracted to someone who cannot give all of themselves because they find this difficult too. This is often why a relationship with a lover seems perfect, and the lovers may dream of being together, only to find that everything collapses if the affair comes to light and they move in together. To be blunt, the relationship between the lover and partner may not succeed because it cannot take the togetherness that the relationship needs. They may also feel as if the relationship has been built on a deception, and this can be hard to cope with psychologically. Or it may be that the lover never meant the relationship to be 'full on' and now finds themselves reluctantly drawn into a commitment they never intended to make. They may have enjoyed the excitement and illicit thrill of a relationship built on snatched encounters or fast passionate sex, but cannot hack the reality of television dinners and a partner who snores.

THE WAITING LOVER

A lover may live on promises, hoping that their partner will leave their husband or wife to come and be with them. Some people, frequently women, find themselves living 'shadow' lives, enduring lonely Christmases and birthdays. In my experience of Relate counselling I would say that if a person is going to leave a relationship they will usually do so within nine months of the affair beginning. After this time, unless the affair is revealed, they are likely to stay with the triangle as it is. This is usually because they are gaining something valuable from the situation – perhaps a bolt hole from daily stresses, confirmation of their sexuality, or a need not to see themselves as committed to just one person.

If you do decide to make a relationship together it can be helpful to have a gap between moving from one relationship to the other. This will give you breathing space and a chance to get to know each other without the pressure of deception, and in the real world. Do some ordinary things together – like shopping and cooking – to help you develop a relationship that feels more open and less in 'a bubble'.

THE SAME-SEX LOVER

Sometimes an individual in a heterosexual partnership may have an affair with a same-sex partner because they cannot admit to this side of their sexuality in their everyday life. Although many of the remarks already made about affairs apply to these relationships, they can cause many problems once revealed because of the prejudices some people have about same-sex partnerships. They can also be difficult for the committed partner, who may feel as if their own sexuality is under attack and that they were 'not good enough' for their partner. The subsequent slump in self-esteem can be made worse by the feeling that they lived a lie with a partner who may be gay or bisexual.

THE LOVER'S PERSPECTIVE

Some lovers reason that a secret affair can do no harm to a committed relationship and so carry on the affair, but this is not true. Every affair has an effect on a couple, whether the affair is revealed or not. This can be true even if the affair is kept a secret for years. The very fact that the deception occurred subtly changes the way in which the couple relates to one another. The person who has the affair may hide aspects of themselves or feel less close to their partner. Over a long period of time, this can make a real difference to a relationship and gives the lie to the notion that what is not known cannot harm.

The lover's role is often one of great difficulty. Frequently, and inaccurately, completely blamed for the affair, they may also experience as much confusion about what lies ahead as the couple. Much of the information in this chapter about talking about the affair with a committed partner will be true for the lover. He or she also deserves the relationship to be assessed or ended in a way that gives time for consideration and reflection, rather than ending in a row after the affair becomes publicly known. Some people who find they are a lover to a person in a committed relationship never intend the pain that the affair causes. It is important to remember that all the people in an affair triangle are attempting to cope with the effects of an affair.

This chapter has been about making decisions about going on together. At the right time, telling others is an important part of making this assessment because you may need their support as you try to move forward or split up. Handling this issue with due sensitivity towards your partner and others demonstrates maturity and care that may help to lessen the negative results of the affair. It can also help you to communicate successfully with a partner in order to decide what lies ahead for the two of you.

AFTERWORD

The aim of this book has been to help you understand the nature of trust, what causes affairs and how to manage the fallout from an affair.

It is not unusual for the media to say that affairs can improve a relationship or are transitory and therefore not important. This is not the case. Most affairs cause problems that add to already difficult situations. They are not cures, but part of the disease in an unhappy relationship.

I hope that through reading this book you will understand more about the effect affairs have on ordinary people's lives. Especially, I hope that you have been helped by it, whether you have read the book because you have had an affair, been the partner of someone who has had an affair or observed the affair of a friend or member of your family.

You will have learnt that the effect of an affair can last a long time, but that affairs do not always spell the end of the relationship. With hard work and patience your relationship can come through an affair, changed but often strengthened.

The key message of this book is that affairs happen for a variety of reasons and that as a couple you need to engage with, not run away from, the reasons for the affair. If you can do this and decide to stay together, you will have a relationship that is able to stand up to pressure in the future. If you part, you will know you were not afraid to face the truth about what caused the affair and be better prepared for the future and any relationship that is waiting round the corner.

I wish you all you would wish for yourself in your relationships, now and in the future.

FURTHER HELP AND READING

Relate is here for people who want to make their family relationships better. We help people make sense of what's happening in their relationships, decide what they want to do and make those changes.

In addition to our respected and popular range of books, we have many other ways to support people. Our counsellors are trained professionals. You can have a local appointment with a counsellor face-to-face, on the phone or consult them online through our website. We also run counselling for children in primary and secondary schools, family counselling, and education and learning courses.

We work with couples, families and individuals. Our network reaches across England, Wales and Northern Ireland, where we are the largest provider of relationship support and sex therapy.

Find more relationship advice and information about our services on our website at www.relate.org.uk or call us on 0300 100 1234.

HELPLINES

Relate: 0300 100 1234

National Mediation: 0845 60 30 809

National Domestic Violence Helpline: 0808 2000 247

Parentline Plus: 0808 800 2222

Samaritans: 08457 90 90 90

BOOKS

Relate books, especially:
How to have a Healthy Divorce, Paula Hall (Vermilion, 2008)
Help Your Children Cope with Your Divorce, Paula Hall (Vermilion, 2007)
Moving On, Suzie Hayman (Vermilion, 2001)
Loving Yourself, Loving Another, Julia Cole (Vermilion, 2001)

WEBSITES

www.relate.org.uk
Relate offers advice, relationship counselling, sex therapy, workshops, mediation, consultations and support, face to face, by phone and through their website.

www.relationships-scotland.org.uk
Relationship counselling and family support across Scotland.

www.samaritans.org
Emotional support 24 hours a day.

www.directgov.gov.uk
A general public service site that provides legal information on separation and divorce.

www.MIND.org.uk
The UK's national association for mental health.

www.parentlineplus.org.uk
A national charity with decades of experience of supporting parents and carers via a range of free, flexible, innovative services.

www.pinktherapy.com
The UK's largest independent therapy organisation working with gender and sexual minority clients.

www.respect.uk.net
National association of domestic violence perpetrators programmes. Provides information and help for perpetrators of domestic violence.

www.ukcfm.co.uk
The website of the UK College of Family Mediators. Provides information on family mediation and information on regional mediation services.

www.womensaid.org.uk
A national domestic violence charity that provides support, advice and temporary accommodation to women and men affected by violence or abuse.

INDEX

223

Starting Again

Sarah Litvinoff

When a relationship finishes it can feel like the end of the world, but it is also a new beginning. In *Starting Again*, Sarah Litvinoff looks at the lessons that can be learnt from a relationship that has ended and helps you to deal with your feelings of separation, grief and recovery.

Through self-assessment questionnaires, tasks and discussion points you will reach a greater understanding of yourself and your relationships and be able to start looking to a positive future. This book will help you to come to terms with the ending of a relationship and assess what went wrong, become aware of and break patterns you have unconsciously repeated, start again and build a new social life for yourself.

£7.99   ISBN 9780091856670

How to Have a Healthy Divorce

Paula Hall

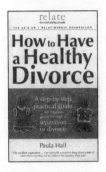

The process of divorce can be an emotionally devastating experience and the financial and legal strains can be a major source of stress. But approaching divorce with the right advice and support can help you turn the experience into a chance for personal growth and development, so you can look to the future with a realistic optimism.

How to Have a Healthy Divorce will help you to embrace the reality of the situation, gain more understanding of what went wrong and help you handle the rollercoaster of emotions involved. In clear and simple steps, this practical guide will show you how to:

- Overcome actual and potential challenges
- Accept your past, present and future circumstances
- Formulate a personal action plan that includes practical points on financial and legal matters
- Build a relationship with your ex so you can communicate effectively

This accessible, sympathetic and uncomplicated guide will help you to emerge from a healthy divorce with valuable lessons learnt and the tools to build a secure and fulfilling future.

£9.99   ISBN. 9780091924003

Order this title direct from www.rbooks.co.uk

The Relate Guide to Finding Love
Barbara Bloomfield

Why are you looking for love right now? What kind of relation-ship do you want? How will you know when you've found 'The One'? *The Relate Guide to Finding Love* will answer all these questions, and more.

From the UK's leading relationship counsellor, *The Relate Guide to Finding Love* offers common-sense help and advice on all aspects of dating and relationships. Short, snappy chapters, each containing a thought-provoking exercise, plus personal case histories, combine to make this a fun and interesting read to help you to:

- Discover your needs and what you expect from a relationship
- Get yourself into the right frame of mind to meet someone new
- Make the most of online dating and singles events
- Identify whether your new love is really the one for you

Whether you are looking for a long-term relationship or just a quick fling, this practical, accessible guide is perfect for you.

£9.99   ISBN 9780091923976

Order this title direct from www.rbooks.co.uk